THE MAKING OF
DRAGONHEART

THE MAKING OF DRAGONHEART

Jody Duncan

BOULEVARD BOOKS
NEW YORK

THE MAKING OF DRAGONHEART

A Boulevard Book / published by arrangement with
MCA Publishing Rights, a Division of MCA, Inc.

PRINTING HISTORY
Boulevard edition / June 1996

The Putnam Berkley World Wide Web site address is
http://www.berkley.com

ISBN: 1-57297-109-6

BOULEVARD
Boulevard Books are published by The Berkley Publishing Group,
200 Madison Avenue, New York, New York 10016.
BOULEVARD and its logo are trademarks
belonging to Berkley Publishing Corporation.

PRINTED IN THE UNITED STATES OF AMERICA

10 9 8 7 6 5 4 3 2 1

Book design by H. Roberts Design

ACKNOWLEDGMENTS

There is something magical about this dragon.

Over and over again, as I interviewed the people involved in the making of *Dragonheart*, I had down-to-earth, seasoned filmmakers tell me that this production was like no other; that it meant more than most; that there was something, well, *magical* about it.

My own involvement was, of course, only peripheral; but I, too, had an experience that was unique. Rather than the perfunctory thirty-minute interview that I am often granted by the busy director, Rob Cohen spent a total of nine hours with me, revealing not only the happy stories that would make their way into press releases, but also the struggles, the self-doubts, the human dramas that were all a part of the making of *Dragonheart*.

Producer Raffaella de Laurentiis was equally forthcoming, and her inherent charm and intelligence made my interview with her one of the most enjoyable of my career.

Over coffee, Dennis Quaid proved to be as funny, generous and insightful as his *Dragonheart* coworkers had promised.

Writer Charles Edward Pogue invited me into his home, where throughout a long morning he spoke with wit and wisdom about screenwriting in general, and *Dragonheart* in particular.

At Industrial Light & Magic, I was given the opportunity to sit in on dailies, during which time I viewed footage of Draco the dragon that was nothing less than spectacular. Visual effects supervisor Scott Squires then followed up with an hours-long phone call in which he patiently went through the movie shot by shot, explaining each of the computer-generated effects in detail.

Also generous with their time and insights were Phil Tippett, Kit West, Benjamin Fernandez, John Swallow, David Thewlis and Dina Meyer.

Thank you, all, for your invaluable contributions to this book.

My thanks, as well, to Nancy Cushing-Jones and Debra Mostow Zakarin for entrusting me with the project.

Finally, love and thanks to my sisters, Pamela and Margie, with whom I share one heart.

INTRODUCTION

t his is the story of one man, one dragon and one heart.

It is the tenth century and the world has not yet been tamed. An unrestrained Nature is evident in the weed-pocked wildness of the wheat fields, the jagged peaks of the mountains and the coarse spirits of the horses and pigs and pack dogs that roam free in vast, overgrown forests.

Mankind is insignificant against Nature's unbridled grandeur. Along riverbanks there are, here and there, crude huts joined together in informal community—but these pockets of humanity are too tenuous, too barbaric to be called civilization.

One who tried to make this raw world civilized, King Arthur, is long dead, as are the principles by which he ruled. Might is, once again, Right, and only the most stalwart of idealists remember the old code: *A knight is sworn to valor; his heart knows only virtue; his blade defends the helpless; his might upholds the weak; his word speaks only truth; his wrath undoes the wicked!*

It is a time when dragons walk the earth. Ancient and wise, the creatures had, in days past, generously bestowed upon Mankind the gifts of music and art and language. But once possessing those treasures, Man, in his arrogance, had spurned the dragons' gentle ways and set out on his own ruinous path. Now, Mankind and the last surviving dragons coexist in mutual distrust and suspicion.

It is in this world that Bowen, a knight of the old code, lives.

Dearest to Bowen is Prince Einon. Both pupil and surrogate son to the idealistic knight, the young prince dutifully parrots Bowen's lessons in honor; but his words mask a cruel ambition. Mortally wounded in a peasant uprising, Einon is delivered to a dragon's cave, where his mother, Queen Aislinn, implores the beast to apply some magical remedy. Hoping that through a magnanimous gesture he might mend the rift between dragon and Man, the creature opens his chest and offers one-half of his glowing heart of light and fire. With the dragon's sacrifice, Einon's wounds are instantly healed.

But the evil in the boy thrives still. With his ascent to the throne, Einon proves to be a savage, vengeful king. Believing that the dragon's heart has poisoned his precious boy, Bowen leaves the young king's service, vowing to slay every last dragon on earth.

Fourteen years pass. A dragonslayer by trade, Bowen, now cynical and disillusioned, has nearly made good on his promise. Only one dragon remains, a melancholy beast named Draco who is weary of the never-ending succession of dragonslayers who chase him from field to stream to mountain and back again. Bowen, too, chases him down. But

after a furious battle and a long, futile standoff, both dragon and knight recognize the pointlessness of their rivalry. A pact born of pragmatism is formed, and the unlikely colleagues set off to work a profitable scam from village to village.

Gradually, the strained tolerance between knight and dragon gives way to deep feelings of affection, respect and comradeship. Through his friendship with Draco and the passionate influence of Kara—a spirited peasant girl—the dim fire of Bowen's honor is rekindled. With dragon banners flying, Bowen leads a revolution against King Einon that ends with Draco's capture and the revelation of a terrible truth: The beloved dragon and the wicked king, sharing the same heart, are mortally connected, and only through Draco's death can Einon be destroyed. Having found a sublime purpose to his life, Draco implores Bowen to kill him, and thus put an end to Einon's tyranny. In anguish, the knight commits the act, his heavy heart uplifted as he witnesses the ascent of Draco's glorious spirit to the heavens.

Bringing this heroic tale to the screen required behind-the-scenes heroics not commonly found within the machinations of film production. For more than seven years, producer Raffaella de Laurentiis fought for *Dragonheart* with maternal fierceness, believing in the project even when told flatly that a movie starring a talking dragon could not be realized. Over and over again, the producer's dedication breathed life into the project as it nearly died a thousand deaths in development.

Dragonheart was finally given a green light by Universal Pictures in 1994; but still, the struggle did not end. Director Rob Cohen, with only one major feature under his belt, was faced with delivering one of the most complex and technically daunting films in the studio's history. A composite tenth-century world had to be created; large-scale practical fire effects, vital to a film about a fire-breathing dragon, had to be staged; most significantly, Draco had to be realized—entirely through visual effects techniques—as a character of depth and charm.

With de Laurentiis and Cohen, a dedicated, talented team of designers, cinematographers, actors and visual and special effects technicians labored for nearly five months in the alien atmosphere of a postcommunist, Eastern European country. Away from home, in a location that was, both geographically and culturally, far removed from Hollywood, the crew shot 95 days of its 104-day principal photography schedule outdoors, braving precipitous, cliffside locations and weather that ranged from the record-breaking heat of summer to the numbing, below-zero temperatures of winter.

Even with the end of the arduous three-and-a-half-month shoot, another full year of postproduction was required to realize the computer-generated (CG) effects through which Draco would be portrayed. For *Dragonheart*, the visual effects artists at Industrial Light & Magic reached well beyond the parameters they had themselves set with their work for Steven Spielberg's *Jurassic Park* in order to create a CG character of unprecedented complexity.

Dragonheart, the movie that was nearly a decade in the making, was released in summer 1996. It came at the tail end of a wave of sword-and-sorcery films that were released as the genre enjoyed a resurgence of popularity. But although it was the latecomer, the film offered something rarely seen in the annual deluge of big-budget summer movies: a story of mythic proportions told with fablelike simplicity; a story celebrating honor, sacrifice and friendship; a story of one man, one dragon and one magnificent heart.

PREPRODUCTION

"Their attitude was, 'You want to make a movie about a talking dragon? Are you kidding?'"
—Raffaella de Laurentiis

In 1988, Patrick Read Johnson, a visual effects artisan and aspiring writer and filmmaker, had an idea for a film that was so beautiful and powerful, it would capture the imaginations of nearly all who heard it for many years to come. A young director with only one low-budget film, *Spaced Invaders,* to his credit, Johnson was nonetheless confident that his premise was surefire movie material, and he began pitching it to anyone willing to sit and listen.

One who was willing was producer Raffaella de Laurentiis. A respected filmmaker who had shown a proclivity for orchestrating complicated productions in foreign locations, de Laurentiis—the daughter of producer Dino de Laurentiis—had begun working in the film industry at the age of fifteen, assisting in the prop and set dressing departments and eventually advancing to art direction and costume design. As she matured, de Laurentiis moved into production, acting as a production assistant for her father's film *Hurricane*, and finally as a full-fledged producer for 1982's *Conan the Barbarian*. From there, de Laurentiis went on to produce *Dune*, *Conan the Destroyer* and *Tai-Pan*, finally starting her own company, Raffaella Productions, in 1988. A year later, de Laurentiis's fledgling company produced its first feature, *Prancer*.

It was about the time of *Prancer*'s release that de Laurentiis was introduced to the story that would become *Dragonheart*. "Patrick Johnson came to me with a seed of an idea about this world inhabited by dragons," de Laurentiis recalled. "The dragons were very savvy. They knew language and mathematics and art. Then Man came along and the dragons taught Man everything they knew; and, as usual, as soon as Man got the knowledge, he started slaughtering the dragons. Patrick's story actually picked up in a world in which there are only twenty-five or thirty dragons left, and Man has taken over. Finally, it comes down to the last dragon and the last dragonslayer, who start out as enemies but become friends. It was a great yarn, and I fell in love with it immediately."

The producer was so enamored with the story, in fact, that she began an enthusiastic campaign on its behalf, pitching it to every movie studio in town. "Unfortunately, no studio would buy it," de Laurentiis said. "Their attitude was, 'You want to make a movie about a talking dragon? Are you kidding?' So I got absolutely nowhere with it. But, even so, I could never get it out of my head. I would tell the story to my nieces and nephews and they would listen, enraptured, for an hour or more. That, as much as anything, convinced me that it was a great idea, and that my instincts about what kind of movie it would make were right."

Discouraged by the studios' response, but still determined, de Laurentiis continued to approach directors and production executives, and in an extraordinary act of faith, even went so far as to buy the rights to the project out of her own pocket. "That is not the kind of thing you want to do in this town," de Laurentiis said, laughing. "But when everyone said no, I

thought to myself that I *couldn't* let it go to another producer. There was nothing to do but buy the rights myself. That's how passionate I was about it."

What de Laurentiis had purchased was, at this point, not much more than a nebulous idea. Although Patrick Johnson carried a broad outline of the story in his head and heart, nothing resembling a real screenplay had yet been committed to paper. It was not until two years later, when Johnson met screenwriter Charles Edward Pogue through their mutual manager that *Dragonheart* would find its voice.

Pogue had started his screenwriting career penning adaptations of Sherlock Holmes stories for British television, and had gone on to write intelligent, well-received screenplays for *Psycho III, D.O.A.* and David Cronenberg's remake of *The Fly*. In Pogue, both Johnson and de Laurentiis felt they had found a writer who had the talent and the sensibilities necessary to transform Johnson's vague notion into a full-fledged screenplay.

The screenwriter needed little in the way of convincing before he committed whole-heartedly to the task. "Patrick came to me and said that he had this idea about a dragon and a knight," Pogue recalled, "and I said, 'Stop right there—I'll do it.' My favorite movie in the world is *The Adventures of Robin Hood* with Errol Flynn. I love those kinds of movies—the swashbuckler with witty repartee over crossed blades. Patrick went on to explain some of this story he had, and I immediately saw the possibilities in it."

Shortly afterward, Pogue and Johnson began to meet regularly to explore those possibilities. In the course of a fruitful two-week period, a basic outline for the screenplay was fashioned. "What Patrick had was a beginning and an end," Pogue commented, "but not much in the middle. So we began to work on it, incorporating Patrick's ideas. One of the things he wanted to do was weave in the whole Arthurian myth, but in an oblique way, with references to the old code and the tor, the mythical burial ground of King Arthur at the castle of Avalon. After Patrick and I worked out the outline, I sat down to write the screenplay."

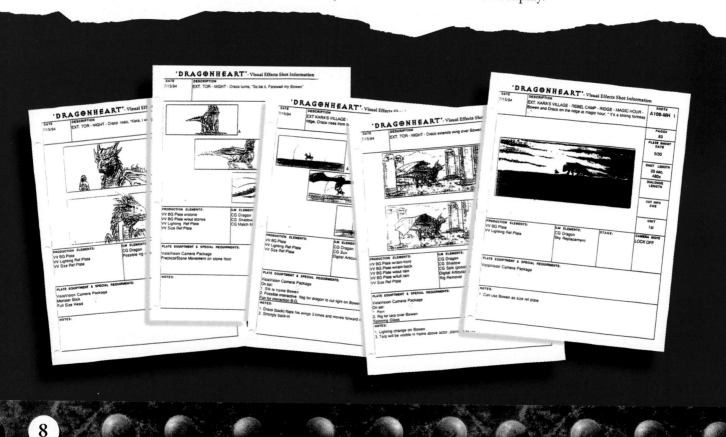

Thematically, what Pogue saw in *Dragonheart* as he began to write was a story about a disillusioned man's struggle to recapture his idealism. "Often in my writing I will start out with a flawed character, someone who has lost his way and is trying to regain it," said Pogue. "That was the appeal to me in Bowen's character. Kara is just the opposite—she is all passion and fire and ideals. In fact, Bowen says to her at one point, 'In you, I see myself once upon a time.' That is why these two people connect so fiercely. The theme that seemed to fall very naturally into place with this story was the attempt to maintain one's passion in the cesspool of the world." Developing the character of Draco also came fairly easily to the screenwriter. "I tended to think of Draco as a human being, rather than a dragon, and I wrote lines for him accordingly. Draco's voice and personality gelled immediately."

While the character of Draco evolved quickly, the detailed back story regarding dragon culture and spiritual afterlife presented Pogue with one of the script's major challenges. "The mythology of the dragons, in general, and Draco's subtext and drive in particular were very difficult to work out. The trouble I had in writing the back story was figuring out why Draco hangs on. He is in despair, all of his brethren are gone—why doesn't he just let Bowen slay him and be done with it? I had to give him a reason to be afraid to die. So I came up with the idea of his guilt over the fact that he has given half his heart to the wrong person. He has made a dreadful mistake in bestowing the gift on Einon; and if he dies, he fears he will go soulless into Hell.

"But then he links up with Bowen and he sees some hope. He thinks maybe this is the guy through which he can redeem himself, not knowing that the ultimate sacrifice is coming down the road—that he must die in order for Einon to die. The one choice he dreads most is the choice he has to make in order for him to reach the stars and be with his brothers."

One by one, each major story issue was resolved; and after only two months, Pogue had completed his first draft of the *Dragonheart* screenplay. "The script flowed," Pogue marveled. "It was like white heat. It just came to me, and it all crystallized very quickly. I'd never had a writing experience that was pure joy from beginning to end, but that's what writing *Dragonheart* was like."

Revisions of that first draft were executed by Pogue, Patrick Johnson and Raffaella de Laurentiis in a weeklong brainstorming session, during which time the threesome went through the script page by page, line by line. When it was over, ten pages had been cut. "Raffaella's gift as a producer is that she is great in the editing process," Pogue observed. "She can cut ten pages and you will never miss them. She also has a very good story sense; she understands continuity and through-line." What de Laurentiis had in her possession at the end of the revision process was a tangible representation of the story she had embraced so enthusiastically two years earlier—a screenplay that was both an exciting adventure and a romantic fairy tale.

To Pogue, the story he had fashioned into screenplay form was also something of a fable for our times. "I think people are looking for something to renew their idealism and their faith in the world," Pogue reflected. "I think people feel as if they have lost their moral center. We've all become blame-shifters and crybabies, and nobody wants to take responsibility. *Dragonheart,* to me, was in part about reaching beyond that. This story says, 'We must deal with life as it is; but we can't lose sight of life as it *should* be.'"

With the completion of the script, de Laurentiis was able, at long last, to secure a commitment from Universal Pictures to put *Dragonheart* into official development. It was an encouraging nod from a major, powerhouse studio, and de Laurentiis began to hope that her little movie was going to be made after all. But, as she would soon learn, there was still a long

"All through this I was thinking, 'I shouldn't get too involved, because this project is never going to come to me. The studio is dealing with heavy hitters—and I'm just making this kung-fu biography film.'"
—Rob Cohen

road to travel before even a single camera would roll in service to *Dragonheart*.

 Dragonheart was coming along. The project could now boast a screenplay, a development deal with Universal and the studio's tentative agreement to go with Patrick Johnson as director. Glaringly absent, however, was the dragon. As conceived by Chuck Pogue, Draco was a talking, flying, singing, philosophizing, fire-breathing creature who, with the actor pegged to portray Bowen, would carry the movie on his imaginary shoulders. The creation of Draco was a daunting prospect that had, in large part, accounted for many a filmmaker's reluctance to take on the project.

 After nearly one hundred years of moviemaking and special effects development, the options available for realizing fantasy characters were still limited to variations on stop-motion animation, animatronics or human performers in elaborate suits. Stop-motion—developed by Willis O'Brien in 1915, and subsequently showcased in full-length features such as 1925's *The Lost World* and 1933's *King Kong*—is a time-honored process in which a miniature puppet is positioned and filmed one frame at a time. Subtly refined through the years by such renowned animators as Ray Harryhausen, Jim Danforth and Phil Tippett, the process has essentially remained the same since O'Brien's first crude experiments, and telltale glitches are still detectable in the final imagery. As extraordinary as the effect was in its time, increasingly sophisticated audiences have long since come to recognize stop-motion for the cinematic trickery that it is. In addition, the technique is excruciatingly time-consuming, and therefore expensive. For all of these reasons, stop-motion did not seem a viable option for creating a character that would be featured in nearly every scene of *Dragonheart*.

A high-tech variation of the technique, dubbed "go-motion," was devised and implemented by Phil Tippett for the 1981 film *Dragonslayer.* Instead of the animator moving the armatured character one frame at a time, the puppet was mounted to a motion-control rig that could execute broad moves—such as the flapping of wings—with reliable repeatability. Go-motion produced animation with a realistic motion blur, and the jerky movements so common to stop-motion were virtually eliminated. Still, like its predecessor, go-motion was expensive and cumbersome.

Animatronics technology, used to create full-scale mechanical characters, also had its limitations. Animatronic characters such as those created by Stan Winston for *Aliens* and both *Terminator* movies had admirably supported those films' practical and computer-generated effects; even so, they had been used to best advantage in quick, forgiving cuts. No one involved in *Dragonheart*'s development gave credence to the notion that a full-scale, animatronic Draco could adequately convey the character for the entire length of the film. For obvious reasons, the men-in-suits idea was even less appealing.

Assuming that Draco would have to be achieved through some form of puppetry, Universal commissioned a million-dollar test from the renowned Jim Henson's Creature Shop in London, where a full-size dragon head was built and put through its paces. Although the Henson device was state-of-the-art, Universal executives were not convinced that *any* kind of puppet could be expected to portray the magical Draco. The question of how the dragon would be achieved remained unanswered as development ground to a halt.

It was about this time that the project hit yet another snag. The studio had agreed to go with the inexperienced Patrick Johnson as director as long as the movie could be made for under $15 million. But no matter how aggressively she crunched her numbers, de Laurentiis could not come up with a budget for the movie that totaled less than $21 million. "Even that wasn't a realistic sum," the producer admitted. "This was too big a movie with too many effects to be done on that small a budget. So eventually the studio said, 'We love the script, and we want to do it. But if it is going to be a big-budget production, we want a major director involved.' It was understandable. Patrick is enormously talented—he went on to great success as a director—but he was very young, and only had one little movie to his credit at the time. Still, Patrick was the guy who had the original idea, and you can never take that away from him."

The split with Johnson was an amicable one, and his peripheral involvement in the project was ensured with his agreement to act as *Dragonheart*'s executive producer. Johnson would also receive story credit on the film.

In response to the studio's mandate, de Laurentiis went looking for a big-name director. "We got tremendous response from a lot of really talented directors," she commented. "Kenneth Branagh was involved for a while; Richard Donner wanted to do it, as well." Donner's enthusiasm for the project was so high, in fact, that he was in development with *Dragonheart* for a full six months before deciding to move on to other projects.

Two important events happened in the meantime that would prove to have a significant impact on *Dragonheart.* The first was the release of Steven Spielberg's *Jurassic Park,* a movie about genetically engineered dinosaurs that would become the highest-grossing film in motion picture history. In large part, its success was due to the amazing dinosaurs themselves—creatures that were created through new computer graphics technology. Here, at last, was a means by which Draco could be realized in all his glory.

Surprisingly, de Laurentiis did not make the connection to her own pet project when first viewing *Jurassic Park.* "I didn't think about *Dragonheart* at all," she admitted. "I just saw that first shot of the dinosaur and I got tears in my eyes. I was really moved by the fact that I worked

in an industry that could create something so spectacular. It wasn't until later that it occurred to me that we could create Draco in the same way." Although it was notoriously expensive, Universal agreed that CG was the way to go—and with a new estimated budget of $57 million, the little *Dragonheart* project was suddenly launched into the arena of big effects films.

The other significant event that occurred as the *Dragonheart* project faltered in development was de Laurentiis's pairing with director Rob Cohen for the making of *Dragon: The Bruce Lee Story*. Cohen had served as executive vice president of Motown's motion picture division and was behind such films as *Mahogany* and *The Wiz*. He made his directing debut with *A Small Circle of Friends* for United Artists, then went on to a successful television career, directing episodes of *Miami Vice*, *A Year in the Life* and *thirtysomething*, as well as a number of commercials. Cohen kept his hand in feature films while honing his television directing skills, executive-producing *The Razor's Edge*, *The Witches of Eastwick*, *The Running Man*, *Ironweed*, *The Serpent and the Rainbow* and *Light of Day*. In 1988, Cohen joined with director John Badham to form The Badham/Cohen Group. The company's first production was *Bird on a Wire*, followed by *The Hard Way*.

It was during his tenure with Badham that Cohen first came into contact with *Dragonheart*. Hoping to interest Badham in the project, de Laurentiis had sent the script to the director. A few weeks later, it was Cohen, not Badham, who called to respond to her overture. "Rob called me and said how much he loved the script, that it was one of the best scripts he'd ever read," de Laurentiis recalled. "But he said that Badham wasn't interested because he didn't want to do a big effects movie. So nothing came of it at the time. Later on, I was struck by the irony of it—that the first conversation I ever had with Rob was regarding *Dragonheart*."

"I was totally captivated by the script," Cohen commented. "I thought the story was quite beautiful, and that it had some lovely, unexpected turns. I told Badham that I thought it was a really good piece of work and that he should do it. But he was very worried about how the dragon could be done. Would it be a Muppet, or what? I had no idea myself."

Cohen had dissolved his partnership with Badham by the time he reconnected with de Laurentiis for *Dragon: The Bruce Lee Story*. The making of the film, directed by Cohen and produced by de Laurentiis, proved to be a mutually satisfying experience for the filmmakers, and by

the time production had come to a close, an unofficial partnership had been formed. "I built up a really good working relationship with Rob during *Dragon*," de Laurentiis commented. "There was a real bond between us. I knew what he needed, and he knew I would give it to him without even discussing it." The success of the pairing became most obvious when *Dragon* was released. While the studio had held only modest expectations for the relatively low-budget film, *Dragon* surprised everyone when it became a box-office hit that grossed more than $35 million. Even more remarkable, considering its subject matter, the film was also well received by critics. Together, de Laurentiis and Cohen had pulled off a major filmmaking coup.

Despite this solid success, however, Cohen—by his own estimation—was still not in the directing big leagues. Because of the complexity of the film, and the tremendous amount of money the studio had committed to its making, Cohen held out little hope that *Dragonheart* would ever be awarded to him. "Throughout the making of *Dragon* I would hear what was going on with *Dragonheart*," Cohen said. "All through this I was thinking, 'I shouldn't get too involved, because this project is never going to come to me. The studio is dealing with heavy hitters—and I'm just making this kung-fu biography film.' I was very happy to be making that film, and I was proud of it, so I thought I should just accept my lot in life and not keep wishing for what I couldn't have."

But then, fate—and a determined producer—stepped in. When negotiations with a number of big-name directors continued to fall through, an exasperated de Laurentiis took a stand. "Raffy went to the studio and said, 'Either give me the project back or let's go forward with Rob,'" recalled Cohen. "She said, 'I don't want to sit in this Nowhere Hell any longer. You have the technological sequel to *Jurassic Park* sitting in your backyard and you're not doing anything with it. We have the chance to take this new CG technology to its next level. Let's do it!'" The impassioned plea was heard loud and clear by the studio—and in January 1994, it was announced that Rob Cohen would be helming Universal's *Dragonheart*.

After some deliberation, Universal agreed to a summer 1996 release, recognizing that even after principal photography was completed, a full year would be required to realize the computer-generated dragon. The schedule roughed out by the filmmaking team mandated a July 1994 start for principal photography. The shoot would wrap at the end of November, and at that time, Cohen would edit the film to as final a form as possible—minus its nearly two hundred dragon shots. Only then would the film finally be delivered to the CG team.

"When the master says, 'That's not enough time,' it makes you rethink things seriously."

—Rob Cohen

Preproduction began officially on January 17, 1994, leaving the production team less than six months in which to prepare for principal photography. "I remember going to see Steven Spielberg about something else," said Cohen, "and he said, 'I hear you're going to do *Dragonheart*. When are you going to shoot?' I said, 'This summer.' He was surprised. 'This summer! How many CG shots do you have?' 'A hundred and seventy-five,' I answered. 'Jeez, we had fifty-seven CG shots in *Jurassic Park*, and I storyboarded for a year!' That was the first time I got scared. When the master says, 'That's not enough time,' it makes you rethink things seriously. But I just didn't have the luxury of time."

Prompted by the time crunch and their shared enthusiasm for the project, Cohen and de Laurentiis immediately threw themselves into a frenzied preproduction. Among the duties that would have to be attended to were final revisions of the script, the assembling of a first-rate team of department heads, the storyboarding of the entire film, location scouting and casting. In addition, sets would have to go under construction weeks in advance of the start of principal photography.

One of the first tasks Cohen tackled after he was charged with the film was the refining of the script with Chuck Pogue. Although Cohen had been among the screenplay's biggest fans, the director felt some minor changes were necessary to make it align more precisely with his overall vision of the film. Specifically, Cohen took the story out of the Robin Hood–era Middle Ages, the twelfth century, and placed it two centuries earlier. "I didn't want women with veiled cones on their heads and men calling them 'wench' and all that sort of thing," Cohen said. "I wanted the story to take place in that period between the collapse of the Roman Empire and the invasion of Normandy, where history picks up again.

It seemed to me that what is commonly called the Dark Ages would be a time when dragons might have lived. That period between the fifth and tenth centuries is very mysterious, and it isn't all that hard to imagine that dragons might have existed then. Nature was still enormous, and in that Nature could be this enormous creature. So this was my thinking when I went back to look at the script. I took it out of a more sophisticated time period and moved it to a time that reflected my rougher vision of the film."

> *"In a sense, we had to make the movie before we made the movie."*
> —Rob Cohen

Another issue that Cohen and Pogue addressed at this juncture was the tightening of the script. Streamlining the number of large-scale action sequences, Cohen felt, would not only save money, it would also make for more economical storytelling. "We couldn't have Bowen and Draco pull off three scams, for example, because it would have been too expensive," Pogue explained. "So we figured out a way to make two scams work as well as three. We also cut the number of battles that were in the script. In streamlining, we actually improved the structure of the story." In the course of these final revisions, the tone of the screenplay was also lightened somewhat. "The first draft had a little darker edge to it," Pogue said. "One of the things Raffaella and I had done early on was go through and excise bloody references; so it wasn't a bloody film at all, but it did have more of a darkness to it. Rob and I agreed that it should be an adult film, but one that kids would also enjoy."

"*Dragonheart*, to me, was essentially a fable," Cohen elaborated, "and fables have a simplicity of narrative, no matter how complex they may be symbolically. As I looked at this story, I saw many levels to it, and I wanted audiences to be able to see those levels. But I also wanted eight-year-olds to be able to look at it and say, 'Oh, Bowen was a good knight; now he's a bad knight; now he's a good knight again.' I wanted a simple telling of the story, with all the complexity working quietly beneath it."

Now generally satisfied with the tone and structure of the script—which would continue to be finessed well into production—Cohen turned his attention to other preproduction matters, such as the assembling of a top-notch team of department heads. That team would include a production designer, director of photography, physical effects supervisor and visual effects supervisor. Aware that de Laurentiis had a roster of experienced people with whom she had worked in her early moviemaking days, Cohen graciously bowed to her instincts in the matter of hiring. "Rob was really great about trusting my judgment when it came to hiring," de Laurentiis remarked. "A lot of directors would say, 'I want my own people!' But Rob said, 'Raffaella, I have never done this kind of movie, so I am going to trust you.' He basically let me assemble this crew. It was a very personal thing for me. I had done a lot of big movies when I was younger and had essentially acted as a producer for my father. During that experience, I had come into contact with all these great European film people. But then, when I started my own company eight or nine years ago, I was making lower-budget pictures, so I was never able to reassemble

that team. They were all top-of-the-line people—and I couldn't afford top-of-the-line people on a little picture like *Prancer*. It was the peak of my career to be able to get all these great people back to do *Dragonheart*. It was a fabulous moment for me, like a homecoming."

Among the first to be engaged was production designer Benjamin Fernandez, with whom de Laurentiis had worked on three previous productions—*Conan, Dune* and *Tai-Pan*. In addition, Fernandez had served as production designer for *Days of Thunder* and *True Romance*. "There are very few people in the business who have the knowledge Benjamin has," de Laurentiis enthused. "He is very talented and experienced, and he knows how to pull off big movies." Fernandez also had a reputation as a master builder, a skill that would be vital for the construction of *Dragonheart*'s tenth-century world. That world would include entire period-style villages, multiple castle sets—both interiors and exteriors—and even a man-made cave and waterfall.

Upon meeting the production designer, Cohen was impressed not only with Fernandez's construction know-how, but also his understanding of the period. "I have found that Americans aren't very knowledgeable about European history and culture," Cohen remarked. "Everything they know seems to come from the movies. For that reason, I thought from the beginning that we would be better off with a European production designer. Benjamin is from Spain, and he had a better feel for the period aspects of this movie. On top of that, he was a wonderful person to work with."

Another key person brought onto the project was director of photography (DP) David Eggby. Cohen and de Laurentiis had been introduced to the Australian cinematographer under rather harrowing circumstances. A mere six days before the commencement of shooting on *Dragon: The Bruce Lee Story*, Cohen had been forced to find a new DP. Eggby, who had been highly recommended, was contacted and agreed to take over the film despite the extremely short notice. "He flew to Hong Kong," de Laurentiis recalled, "and prepped the movie in four days, which was an extraordinary accomplishment. So we knew he was fast, and we knew he was good—especially at big exterior movies. That was important, because *Dragonheart* was going to have a *lot* of exteriors."

"What I learned on *Dragon* was that David is the type of guy who will hang in there with you, no matter what," Cohen elaborated. "He is also open to new ideas, which I appreciate. I am very interested in cinematography, and I have made it my business to learn about it. So I needed someone who wasn't resistant to a technically oriented director. Eggby wasn't at all

resistant. We found on *Dragon* that we spoke the same language. It was a creative collaboration; and I think, as a result, *Dragon* had a very beautiful, unique look to it. When *Dragonheart* came along, I never considered using another DP. I will work with David Eggby every chance I get."

Hired to supervise the film's many practical effects—such as the explosions of dragon fire that would be staged on the sets and outdoor locations—was effects dynamo Kit West. Like Fernandez, West had worked with de Laurentiis on *Dune* and *Tai-Pan*, and was a veteran of such big-scale-effects films as *Raiders of the Lost Ark*, two of the three *Star Wars* movies and *Stargate*.

Despite such a body of experience, West would be confronted with an effects challenge on *Dragonheart* that was, for him, unprecedented. Because so much of the film would involve scenes with a computer-generated character, interactive effects would have to be executed to suggest that character's presence in the live-action plates. If, for example, Draco was scripted to plummet into a lake, water in the lake would have to be made to splash accordingly so that the scene would make sense visually when the computer-generated dragon was inserted later. The creation of such interactive effects would fall to West, and would represent the supervisor's first foray into the demanding realm of digital effects.

By the middle of February, most of the key department heads had committed to the project. At that time, Cohen jumped into an intense storyboarding phase during which he planned every shot in the film down to the last detail. "I had a team of five storyboards artists, and we went to work on a daily basis, talking about the different sequences and how I saw them in my head," Cohen explained. "The artists would draw up my ideas and then I would make suggestions from there. We were very specific in how we laid out these sequences. In a sense, we had to make the movie before we made the movie. We had to completely make it in our heads, and we had to really think it through and commit ourselves—because everything else we did was going to be built around the assumptions we made in these boards. We had some flexibility, of course; but because of the nature of effects shots, and because Draco was in so much of the movie, there wasn't a *lot* of flexibility."

Some twenty notebook binders filled with sketches were accumulated by the time the storyboarding process ended. Those fat, neatly organized binders, which together represented the bible for the making of his movie, were to serve as invaluable guides for Cohen as he continued to prepare for the midsummer shoot.

Throughout all of the planning and storyboarding and hiring, what remained uppermost in the minds of Cohen and de Laurentiis was the issue of where the movie would be shot. In an effort to keep costs down, de Laurentiis—who had made something of a specialty of shooting big productions in difficult foreign locations—explored the option of shooting the movie in Eastern Europe. "Steven Spielberg had just completed *Schindler's List* there," de Laurentiis related, "and he'd had a really good experience. So Rob and I started checking out all these books about Eastern Europe. We discovered a castle in the northern Slovak Republic that looked like something we might be able to use for our Avalon, so we decided to start there." The Slovak Republic had been formed when what was formerly known as Czechoslovakia was split into two countries with the fall of the Soviet Union. "The Czech Republic is the richer country, with big cities and big movie studios; the Slovak Republic is the poorer, more undeveloped one. We didn't know anything about Slovakia—but that's where we headed off to in February."

In Slovakia, de Laurentiis and Cohen met up with unit production manager Milan Stanisic and Benjamin Fernandez to begin scouring the small country for locations. "In a four-

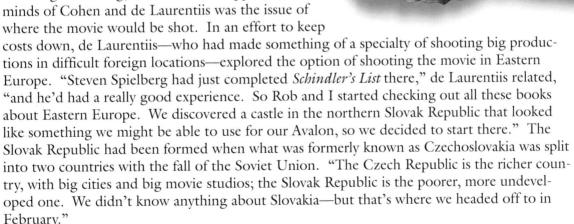

day scout, we found about sixty percent of our locations," Cohen marveled. "Near the city of Spisska, we found our castle for Avalon. It was massive and beautiful, up alone on this hill. It was a grand place. There was the castle itself and an area where we could build our graveyard for the knights of the round table. It was the kind of setting where we could create a very mythical-looking place."

While the Avalon castle had been a relatively easy find, locating a castle to stand in for the stone fortress built by Einon was a frustrating effort. Slovakia was dotted with castles—relics of the region's centuries of defense against the Tartars—but the majority had fallen into ruin and were thus unsuitable for filming. "Most of the castles we looked at were ruins, and *all* of them

were up on these hills and very hard to get to," Cohen noted. "At one point, Benjamin and I were climbing to get to a castle—it was winter and there was snow up to our knees. We were literally climbing from tree root to tree root because the hill was so steep. I lost sight of Benjamin and we wound up on different sides of a slope. Suddenly I heard a scream, 'Ahhh . . . !' It was Benjamin, swearing in every kind of Spanish as he slid down the hill, banging into trees all the way.

"When we finally got up there, we found that this castle was, again, nothing but a ruin. Someone then suggested another castle that was downriver half a mile. So we tramp, tramp, tramp through the snow, and all the while I'm thinking, 'It's going to be another damn ruin.' But then we came around a bend and, like a miracle, there it was. It was three-quarters restored, and it was completely conceivable as the stone castle that Einon builds. Benjamin was very excited. He said, 'All we have to do is build the scaffolding to make it look like Einon is still building it! It is perfect!'" The castle that so captivated Cohen and Fernandez was located in Zilina, in the eastern part of the country. "So now we had Avalon, we had Einon's castle—and everything else fell into place."

In addition to castles, Slovakia was rich with the vast landscapes and expanses of forest that Cohen envisioned for the film. "The agriculture there is very primitive," Cohen said. "It is the only place I've seen in the Western world where people still use ox-drawn wooden plows. There weren't many roads; there weren't jets flying over, leaving contrails. It was quite undeveloped, which was great for our purposes. Slovakia provided all the forests and fields and vistas we needed. There were the beautiful Tatras Mountains as a backdrop, there were grasslands going on to the horizon, there were valleys and streams and castles up on hills. It really suggested a long-ago time period. Through careful location selection, we were able to create the feeling of a very primal world."

Slovakia also provided something that Cohen and de Laurentiis had not expected— a modern, state-of-the-art movie studio. The filmmakers had assumed that studio space for the filming of interiors would have to be uncovered in nearby Prague, in the Czech Republic. In fact, de Laurentiis was preparing to leave Bratislava, the Slovak capital, to look over Prague's facilities when she was approached by locals regarding their own studio. "The people in Bratislava said, 'Wouldn't you like to look at our stages?'" de Laurentiis recalled. "I said, 'I'm sorry, I didn't know you *had* stages.' So the next morning, seven o'clock, they take me to this unbelievable complex! It was Slovensky Film Studio Koliba and it had state-of-the-art soundstages, workshops, offices—everything! It was completely clean, and *empty*. During the Russian regime, they would do twenty or thirty movies a year there, but when the Russians left, the film industry picked up and moved to Prague. So here was this empty studio with everything in perfect working order—and they basically gave me the keys, and I stepped in and had everything for myself. It was fantastic." The studio was not only a more-than-suitable working space, it was a bargain. Whereas stage rental in Hollywood runs between $4,000 and $6,000 per day, the Koliba stages were rented for a mere $300 a day.

"We didn't know anything about Slovakia— but that's where we headed off to in February."
— Raffaella de Laurentiis

"Making an effects film for the first time was like having sex for the first time—I could either grope along like an inexperienced neophyte and hope I got it right, or I could prepare for it by doing my homework."
—Rob Cohen

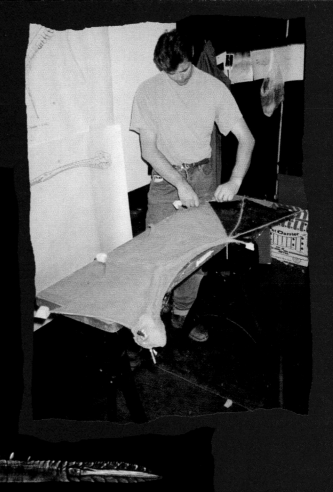

Bratislava became the base of operations for the production, with interior sets such as Draco's cave and the interior of Einon's castle constructed on the Koliba stages. Exterior locations uncovered during the scout—locations in or near the cities of Spisska, Zilina, Martin and Levoca—were all merely hours away. By the time Cohen and de Laurentiis left Slovakia, they were secure in the knowledge that they had found the stages, the forests and the castles in which they would create the tenth-century world of *Dragonheart*.

With key members of their production team in place, and the matter of locations finally settled, Cohen and de Laurentiis turned their attention toward an equally crucial concern—enlisting the visual effects company that would realize Draco. The task of creating the dragon through computer animation would require both artistic skill and an exceptional level of computer graphics sophistication. Although several companies were invited to bid on the project, Cohen leaned toward awarding the film to Industrial Light & Magic (ILM), a group that had won multiple Academy Awards for providing magic in films such as the *Star Wars* and *Indiana Jones* trilogies, *The Abyss*, *Terminator 2*, *Jurassic Park*, *The Mask* and *Casper*.

Universal was as inclined as Cohen toward entrusting *Dragonheart*'s CG shots to ILM. "The studio felt very strongly that it would be a good thing for the film if they could say, 'This movie is created by the visual effects wizards who brought you *Jurassic Park*,'" Cohen noted. "Between their work on *Jurassic* and *Casper*, ILM had delved into two areas that would be very

important to *Dragonheart*. We needed an animal of large scale that could move and fly and act like an animal, like the dinosaurs in *Jurassic*; but we also needed a character that was animated and expressive and could do lip-sync, like the ghosts in *Casper*."

Assigned to oversee ILM's effort on *Dragonheart* was visual effects supervisor Scott Squires, who had just come off supervising the computer effects for *The Mask*. Squires, who had started his career in traditional optical effects and had been in on the ground floor of the facility's burgeoning CG department, had a wide range of experience that made him uniquely qualified to spearhead the effects for *Dragonheart*. Other key personnel were visual effects producer Judith Weaver, a veteran of *The Flintstones* movie; CG supervisor Alex Seiden; and animation supervisor James Straus.

All of the principals at ILM had informally followed *Dragonheart*'s progress for a number of years before the company was awarded the project officially. (During Richard Donner's involvement, in fact, the company had produced a crude dragon test, for which it had modified the computer model of the T-rex featured in *Jurassic Park*.) Finally, in May 1994, ILM signed on to produce the film's effects, and Scott Squires was offered the position of visual effects supervisor.

Before committing to the project, Squires carefully examined both the script and the storyboards. "I could see there was a lot of potential," Squires said. "It was certainly another big leap in terms of technical and creative challenges, and it was a chance to create one of the main characters of a film. So I accepted the project, and left for Slovakia a week later to look at the locations. During a three-week period I met with Rob, David Eggby and Kit West to work out some of the logistical details. Then I came home for a week, had just about enough time to pack and was off to Slovakia again, this time for five and a half months."

With the signing of ILM, Cohen had secured the services of some of the most experienced and talented effects artisans in the film industry. Even so, Cohen—who had no previous experience on an effects film—made a commitment to learn everything he could about effects in general and computer-generated effects in particular. "Making an effects film for the first time was like having sex for the first time," Cohen observed. "I could either grope my way along like an inexperienced neophyte and hope I got it right, or I could prepare for it by doing my homework. By reading everything I could on the subject, I would know what I was doing, at least intellectually, when the big event finally happened. I wanted to understand what the problems were for the CG people, and learn how to avoid them or how to solve them. I read every issue of *American Cinematographer* that had to do with CG. I read *Cinefex*. I read *Video One*. I picked people's brains incessantly. I sat with Scott Squires and asked a lot of questions. I compiled information like a good student; and through that process, I learned how the effects people think. Finally, I began to get it. I couldn't do it myself, but I began to understand the principles, and I knew what I had to capture on film to give them the pieces they needed to create Draco."

Cohen also strengthened his interface with ILM by bringing on visual effects producer John Swallow to act as a liaison between the production and the visual effects. Swallow had met Cohen and de Laurentiis when the effects facility he was working for at the time was asked to bid on the show. He left the company shortly afterward, in part because the company had turned down the invitation. "I was very excited about *Dragonheart* and somewhat disgruntled that they weren't interested in doing it," Swallow commented. "Then, early in May, I got a call from one of the production executives asking me if I'd like to go to Slovakia. I accepted immediately. I think Rob and Raffaella felt they needed someone who was on their side and who understood what was involved in effects. My job was to help coordinate between them, ILM and Kit West."

So important were the practical and visual effects to the overall production that Cohen solicited input from ILM and West during storyboarding. West, in fact, was in on its earliest stages. "I worked right alongside Rob and the storyboard artist," West said, "working out the practical side of the movie, how the practical gags were going to be done. It was great to be involved at that early stage. It is so easy to sketch something, but since I was there, I could tell them if what they had sketched was really a practical idea or not. I'd say, 'Okay, you can do it that way, but it is going to cost you a lot of money. If you do it *this* way, it will cost less.' I think we saved ourselves a lot of expense and trouble down the line because I was in on the planning of the movie so early."

While West concentrated on the live-action aspects of the production, ILM's Judith Weaver, storyboard artist Mark Moore and Steve Price—who was in on the project briefly as visual effects supervisor before Scott Squires took over the assignment—worked with Cohen to board the sequences involving visual effects. Of primary concern were the total number of computer-generated effects shots, each of which would cost the production approximately $100,000. "We had upward of three hundred effects shots at one point," Judith Weaver noted. "It was cost-prohibitive to do that many. So we had this very lengthy and extensive boarding period, and by the time we were through, Rob really had it in his mind how he was going to shoot everything, so he could visualize where we could cut shots. He wanted to avoid typical cheats—the kinds of things that are normally done to cut down the number of effects shots. He was very clever about how he went about it. In most cases, it was just a matter of restaging the action a little bit or making subtle changes in the script. He wound up cutting a hundred and twenty shots without compromising the movie at all."

"After Dennis Quaid left, I turned to Raffy and said, 'You know, that was very much a knight-of-the-old-code kind of thing he just did."
—Rob Cohen

As a result of the revised storyboarding, *Dragonheart* was now trimmed to an ambitious but manageable 182 CG shots. Having set ILM upon the task of creating Draco, Cohen next turned his attention to the casting of the movie's human characters.

Casting the film with casting director Margery Simkin was a process that continued throughout the preproduction period. Everyone's first choice for the vocal performance of Draco was Sean Connery, an actor who, through his long-running portrayal of James Bond and performances in movies such as *Robin and Marian, The Man Who Would Be King* and *The Untouchables*—for which he won an Oscar—had ascended to icon status. Five years earlier, de Laurentiis had sent the script to Connery during the period in which she and Patrick Johnson were first trying to interest major directors and stars in the project. "Sean wanted to do it, even way back then," de Laurentiis noted. "He told me later that he would occasionally call his agent and ask how *Dragonheart* was going—'What happened to that great dragon script?' So when Rob got involved and we approached Sean again, he said, 'Of course! I've always wanted to do it. I'm ready.'"

"Sean Connery *is* a dragon," Cohen noted. "He is a man's man, he's a ladies' man, he's funny. He has wisdom and strength and soul and sexuality, and there is something magical about him. Getting Sean Connery to do the voice of Draco was one of our great victories."

Casting Bowen was a much more arduous task, and was, in fact, the last major issue to be settled before the start of filming. For months, the studio had attempted to interest megastars in the project, and Cohen and de Laurentiis had engaged in long negotiations with a number of those stars' agents and managers, to no avail. "This was basically a road picture with

a guy and a dragon, and most actors didn't relish the thought of playing second fiddle to Draco," Cohen observed. "The reaction was, 'I'm going to be acting against an invisible creature, and I'm going to be in Slovakia like a schmuck for a hundred and four days in 110-degree weather, then Sean Connery is going to go into an air-conditioned recording studio for a few days and he's going to get all the credit because this is the dragon's movie.' It wasn't a very appealing proposition for a lot of actors."

One actor who was not daunted at the prospect of playing Bing Crosby to Draco's Bob Hope was Dennis Quaid. Quaid had first gained attention with his role in 1979's *Breaking Away*, and since then had turned in impressive performances in movies such as *The Long Riders, The Right Stuff, Enemy Mine, The Big Easy, Innerspace, D.O.A.*, and *Wyatt Earp*. Quaid first came into contact with the *Dragonheart* script while at his home in Montana. "I was between projects," Quaid recalled, "so I had my agent send me everything that was going to be shooting in the next six months. I wound up with a stack of about twenty scripts—but *Dragonheart* was the one I thought was really good. I liked its higher themes, the idea of the old code. It was great to see a script that was positive and about virtue, instead of everybody getting killed. *Dragonheart* was on a higher plane. But it was also a great story—it had action and a lot of humor. I remember thinking that it seemed as if it actually could have been written in the tenth century."

After reading the script, Quaid asked his agent to make a call to Rob Cohen. "Dennis's agent, Ed Limato, is someone I have a lot of respect for," Cohen commented. "So when he called to ask what I thought of Dennis Quaid for Bowen, I considered it very seriously. I told him that I really admired Dennis Quaid, and that Raffaella and I would be very happy to talk to him." Shortly afterward, Quaid met with the filmmakers in Cohen's office on the Universal Studios lot. "The first thing that struck me about him was that he is taller than I thought he was," Cohen said. "He is six-one—but he doesn't come across that large on the screen because he is so slim. So right away, I was pleasantly surprised. The kinds of costumes Bowen would be wearing would require a big man to carry off.

"I was even more pleasantly surprised by his attitude. He talked at some length about why he liked the script and why he wanted to do this movie, and Raffy and I were both very

impressed by that. After Dennis Quaid left, I turned to Raffy and said, 'You know, that was very much a knight-of-the-old-code kind of thing he just did. To come into a room and put your case forward is a very brave thing to do—and that's the kind of character we are going to need in an actor.' We knew that a hundred and four days in leather armor on a horse in Eastern Europe was not going to be an easy thing."

Another advantage to Quaid, as de Laurentiis and Cohen saw it, was that the actor had experience doing effects films, and would thus be prepared for the time-consuming, meticulous nature of the shoot. "Dennis had done *Enemy Mine* and *Innerspace*, so he had experience acting with all sorts of technical intervention," noted Cohen.

A quintessentially American actor, the Texas-born Quaid would also keep the film from taking on the highbrow tone of previous sword-and-sorcery films—a tone both de Laurentiis and Cohen wanted to avoid. "A lot of people had suggested that we go with a very sophisticated British actor for Bowen," de Laurentiis said, "but I never wanted an English actor in the role. I never saw the movie as being British, and I didn't want it to have that kind of feeling to it. One of the things I loved about Dennis was the down-to-earth quality he would bring to the movie."

"Dennis had not only proven himself to be a wonderful dramatic actor," Cohen added, "he'd also shown that he is a terrific comedian. The ability to find the humor in this story was very important. We felt Dennis was someone who could do that."

The only drawback, in Cohen's mind, to casting Quaid was that the actor had a decidedly contemporary look. "I needed to be able to imagine him in this time period," Cohen said. "So I talked to Gianetto and Mirella de Rossi, our hair and makeup supervisors, and asked them what they thought about Dennis. Gianetto's response, in a thick Italian accent, was, 'Dennis Quaid—you've got to build up the nobility. Quaid is very American, and Americans are not noble. You people are very nice and friendly, but you're not noble.' So we talked about giving Dennis a beard and longer hair, just to give him a more rugged look and take away that boyish quality of his. I also spoke to our costume designer about coming up with rugged costumes that would add some weight and strength to the character. I began to realize

that with the right costumes and hair and makeup, Dennis Quaid could look very much like he was of the tenth century."

The filmmakers were now convinced that they had found their Bowen. All that remained was to convince the studio. While Universal executives had no reservations about the actor's ability, they did question whether or not Dennis Quaid was a name that could carry a nearly $60 million movie. Cohen and de Laurentiis harbored no such concerns, and from their hotel in Slovakia, they implored the studio to approve their casting choice. "We called the studio and said, 'We want Dennis Quaid,'" Cohen recalled. "'He is the right guy—we can *feel* it.

In our hearts, we know that he is going to be the best Bowen we could ask for. *Please, give us Dennis Quaid.*' This was the very last thing in place: I'd done all the storyboards; I'd done all this preparation; the script had been revised; the budget was done; the locations were all picked; the crew was picked—everything was in place except the actor to play Bowen. A few days after we made that phone call, the studio approved Dennis.

"I had one more conversation with him after that, just to make sure he really wanted to do this. I reminded him that he'd be spending a lot of time on horses. I asked him, 'Do you

like horses?' He said, 'Truthfully, no. Riding is not my favorite thing to do on a Sunday after-noon. But I can do it.' So I said, 'Okay, let's do it.' It was among the smartest things I have ever done."

In addition to Connery and Quaid, a number of first-rate actors were pegged for the film's supporting roles. Cast as Einon was David Thewlis, a respected British actor who had won a best actor award at Cannes for his performance in Mike Leigh's *Naked*. Thewlis had also starred opposite Helen Mirren in PBS's Emmy Award–winning *Prime Suspect III*, and had many television, feature film and stage performances to his credit.

The script was first sent to Thewlis by his agent while the actor was in the United States publicizing *Naked*. "I was reading a lot of big Hollywood scripts at the time," Thewlis recalled, "and I was not inspired by most of them. But I thought that *Dragonheart* had a kind of healthy message behind it. I liked the role of Einon as well, because I enjoy playing compli-cated characters. Bad people are usually the most interesting to play. I thought this movie would give me the chance to do something pretty wild in the characterization, something big and over-the-top."

Having set up an appointment with de Laurentiis and Cohen through his agent, Thewlis went to Universal Studios to meet with the filmmakers toward the end of his four-month whirlwind publicity stint. The meeting never took place. "It had been a wild time," Thewlis recalled, "and by then I was really tired and I just wanted to go home to England. On my way to my first appointment with Rob and Raffaella, I became stuck in traffic, so I was very late. Then I had trouble getting into the studio—there was some kind of problem at the recep-tion desk. Exasperated, I just turned my car around and left. My agent played hell with me for that—'Why didn't you go? Are you crazy? Do you realize who you just missed an appoint-ment with?' I thought, 'Well, I blew that one.' But then a few weeks later they agreed to see me again and give me another chance. Rob was very cool about it. Obviously, he forgave me, because I got the role."

"Thewlis was perfect for Einon," Cohen stated, "because he is the kind of actor who doesn't care if the audience loves him or not. He's very courageous in that way. Thewlis gen-uinely likes exploring the dark side of the soul—even though, as a human being, he is as sweet and gentle a person as one could know. He is also intelligent and well-read and very talented."

Another casting coup for Cohen and de Laurentiis was the signing of Julie Christie to

play the character of Einon's mother, Aislinn. Christie—an Academy Award winner for her performance in 1965's *Darling*—had built a prestigious film career with her subsequent portrayals in *Doctor Zhivago*, *Fahrenheit 451*, *McCabe and Mrs. Miller* and *Shampoo*, but had not accepted an American film role in nearly fifteen years. "We actually got Julie Christie out of retirement," said de Laurentiis. "I asked her at one point why she decided to do *this* movie, after turning down so many others. She said, 'Because it is a fairy tale about good and evil— and the world needs to see this.'"

Thewlis and Christie were represented by the same agent at ICM in London, and before committing, Christie spoke with Thewlis to get his impressions of the project. "Julie loves David," Cohen noted, "so she took his opinion very seriously. I think one of her concerns was

that she didn't know anything about *me*. So, one Sunday morning the phone rang and there was this unmistakable voice on the other end of the line. Julie and I spoke for some time, and at the end of the conversation she agreed to do the movie. I was thrilled to be working with her. I considered it to be a great honor. She always radiates this quality of vulnerability combined with intelligence. I knew she would make Aislinn a wonderful, complex character."

Pete Postlethwaite, a British actor who was nominated for an Academy Award for his dramatic role as Daniel Day-Lewis's father in *In the Name of the Father*—and who subsequently turned in a chilling performance in *The Usual Suspects*— was given the opportunity to flex his comedic muscles as Friar Gilbert, the good-hearted priest and scribe on a quest to find the legendary Avalon. Added to the roster of prestige talent was John Gielgud, who agreed to provide the voice of King Arthur. "One day," de Laurentiis recalled, "I was sitting in my office thinking, 'Well, we got Sean Connery; why not go for John Gielgud?' Rob and Gielgud had worked together years ago, so I just called his agent and said, 'It's two hours' work—will he do it?' And he said yes. We were thrilled."

Unlike the other supporting actors, Dina Meyer—cast as Kara, the rebellious peasant girl—was relatively unknown when she joined the *Dragonheart* cast. Meyer had appeared in a recurring role on *Beverly Hills, 90210* and had also starred with Keanu Reeves in *Johnny Mnemonic*, her feature film debut. Meyer was in the middle of shooting that film in Toronto when she came back to Los Angeles to meet with the filmmakers regarding *Dragonheart*. "I got the impression that they liked me, because Rob wanted to know how long I would be in Toronto and when I would be available to come back in," Meyer recalled. "Sure enough, Rob had me read for him again as soon as we wrapped *Johnny Mnemonic*. Then I read with Dennis Quaid for Rob and Raffaella and the casting director. Dennis and I connected right away, so it was a very easy, comfortable situation. They called my agent immediately after that and said, 'She got it.' It happened very quickly."

What had appealed so immediately to Cohen was Meyer's rough-and-tumble quality. "I wanted a peasant girl," Cohen said. "I wanted someone who looked strong, who looked as if she were capable of doing the kind of hard work peasant girls did in that period. I wanted somebody rooted in the earth. Here is a little girl who has grown up seeing torture and death and enslavement, who feels that the world is wrong and should be put right. Dina suggested those qualities. She is extremely beautiful, but there is nothing fragile about her."

With the signing of Meyer, Cohen had assembled all of his principal actors. It was an impressive group. "I had Dennis Quaid, who, I believe, was meant to play Bowen," Cohen remarked. "I had Sean Connery to give the dragon his voice. On top of that, I had John Gielgud; David Thewlis, a winner at Cannes; Julie Christie, an Academy Award winner; and Pete Postlethwaite, an Academy Award nominee. In addition to Dennis and Sean, we were somehow able to get all of these wonderful people to play our supporting characters."

There was one more crucial role to be "cast." While Sean Connery would provide the voice of Draco, the dragon's physical presence had yet to be determined. To design his leading character, Cohen enlisted Phil Tippett and his Tippett Studio. Since his work on *The Empire Strikes Back*—for which he won an Oscar—and *Dragonslayer,* Tippett had built a reputation as a first-rate creature designer and stop-motion animator. Tippett and his crew had again been honored with an Academy Award for their animation of the dinosaurs in several of *Jurassic Park*'s key scenes.

Dragonheart's dragon would prove to be a tough nut to crack, even for someone of Tippett's experience. "When I called Phil, I told him that the challenge in designing Draco was twofold," Cohen commented. "If we went too far in one direction, he would be too much of a physical creature; and if we went too far in the other direction, he would become Puff the Magic Dragon. The key was to make him anthropomorphic enough so that he would read emotionally, without turning him into a cartoon. His fierceness, his dignity, his power and his mythical qualities all had to be intact—but you also had to be able to look in those eyes and understand what he was feeling, just as you would with any actor. You had to be able to see when he was hurt, when he was being romantic or seductive, charming or sardonic. In order

to do that, Draco had to have a face capable of expressions that we as human beings could interpret."

It was not enough to design Draco merely as a creature with humanlike qualities, however; the dragon also had to possess magical characteristics. "There was an entire mythology we had to create with this creature," Cohen continued. "My thinking was that the dragon was made of fire. The heart that he gives the boy is not a piece of an organ, it is liquid light. Man is dust to dust, but dragons are stardust to stardust. They are made of fire, and that is why they breathe fire and why they can fly. They are not heavy creatures that shake the earth when they walk; they are light and nimble. Draco had to be able to float on his back, swim, fly upside down—all kinds of magical things that a real animal of that size could never do."

Guided by Cohen's input, Tippett and his crew—which included renowned illustrator Doug Henderson and sculptor Pete Koenig—produced a variety of sketches and three-dimensional sculptures over a period of two months. "The way I usually work," Tippett stated, "is that I have an intuitive way I want to go. Then I work with the sculptors here at my studio to come up with ideas. One of the ideas I liked for Draco was based on a Japanese palace guard dog/dragon type of thing. It had a great deal of power in the chest, but it didn't have the typical serpentine neck and long head that we had seen in most dragon designs. I took some sketches of that concept down to L.A. and showed them to Rob. He agreed that we were headed in the right direction, and that it had the right kind of feeling about it. From there, Pete did some sculptures, combining the palace dog concept with a more traditional dragon."

Sean Connery's distinctive facial characteristics were also suggested, subtly, in the dragon's design. "We tried to incorporate Connery as much as possible without doing a caricature of him," Tippett explained. "We had a lot of publicity photos of Connery put up on the walls of our

studio during the sculpting of the face, along with pictures of lions and other creatures that have that similar presence. I think Pete Koenig was very successful in capturing Connery's essence."

Although some of the elements of Draco's design were purely a matter of aesthetics, others addressed physical characteristics mandated by the dragon's actions and behavior in the script. Because the dragon had to be able to express a variety of moods and attitudes, for example, expressive, flexible hands had to be incorporated into the design. Certain size requirements were also dictated by the script's action scenes. One important scene had Bowen positioned inside the dragon's mouth for an extended length of time. To do that, Draco's head would have to be of a size that could accommodate the six-foot-tall actor. "That was a problem," Cohen noted, "because if the head was big enough to fit Dennis Quaid inside, that suggested a certain body size as well. We couldn't get too big with the dragon, though, because we had to build sets he could fit into."

"Man is dust to dust, but dragons are stardust to stardust."
—Rob Cohen

To accommodate the scene while limiting the dimensions of the head, Cohen and Tippett came up with the idea of endowing Draco with snakelike, hinged jaws. "The hinged jaws would enable Draco to eat something much bigger than his own head, just as a boa constrictor can do. We also came up with retractable teeth so that the dragon could look ferocious when he needed to, but still have teeth that were more human-looking when he had to talk. We knew that having a mouth and teeth that were similar to a human's would help the CG animators when it came time to do the lip-syncing."

As the dragon's design evolved, Tippett and Cohen continued to wrestle with the problem of scale, attempting to determine the dragon's exact body size. If the dragon was too large, it would be very difficult for the director to include both Draco and Bowen in the same frame, and the "buddy" component of the buddy film would be severely compromised. A dragon that was too small, however, would lack the majesty and fierceness of the character. To solve the problem, Cohen drew a variety of markings on the side of his house and studied them through a viewfinder to determine what spatial relationships worked best. From those crude framing tests, Cohen and Tippett settled on a three-to-one ratio. Draco would be eighteen feet tall, three times the height of Dennis Quaid. From head to tail, the dragon would measure approximately forty-two feet long.

Another problematic area of the dragon design was the engineering of the wings. "Nature has never designed a quadruped with wings on its back," Tippett noted. "So we were faced with engineering something that would never happen naturally in a hundred million years. Originally, we did calculations to figure out how big the wings would have to be to make something of this size actually fly, and it came out to something like a hundred-and-twenty-five-foot wingspan. But Rob said, 'The wingspan can't be that big! I have a set that is only forty feet wide, and if this thing has a hundred-twenty-five-foot wingspan, it is never going to work!' But if we made them too small, how could the dragon become airborne and not look like a bee—this big fat thing with little tiny wings trying to keep it aloft? It was a problem, and we had to play around with the wing size quite a bit before we found a compromise. In some of the designs, the wings would look great when they were extended and flying, but then when we folded them up against his body, they stuck out too far. A lot of effort went into figuring out what would work functionally, both in a flying mode and a terrestrial mode."

After the major design issues had been ironed out, Tippett and his team produced ten maquettes—small-scale models—and presented them to Cohen at his ranch in Lake Tahoe. "Phil showed up with boxes filled with maquettes," Cohen recalled. "I told him, 'I'm going to leave the room. When you've got them all unpacked and on the coffee table, I'll come back in and see which one catches my eye.' When I came back in and scanned the table, one of them just screamed 'Draco' to me. He was powerful; he was noble; he was regal. He had the bearing of a great creature. He had what Connery has—authority. With that first maquette, Draco was born."

Refinements of the design were implemented in the following weeks. One late idea was a "Swiss Army knife" tail which would transform into a lethal blade during the dragon's fight scenes. The suggestion of an armored, scaled hide was also enhanced with the addition of a shimmering, metallic gold on the wings and spikes covering the dragon's body. "We came up with a lot of refinements and new ideas as we worked," Cohen recalled. "The great thing about working with Phil is that he has such a wonderful imagination. He is a very gifted designer—for every idea I had, he would come up with three new, better ideas."

With the design finally locked, Tippett and his crew produced a number of variously scaled Draco models, including a two-and-a-half-foot-long posable version that the filmmakers could refer to on the set. "This 'posable' model was essentially a crude stop-motion puppet, with an armature and foam latex skin," Tippett explained. "The production team took it with them to Slovakia, and it turned out to be very helpful. It gave them something to position in front of the camera so they could quickly previsualize the action." Three five-foot-long, hard urethane and fiberglass models were also produced. One was kept at the Tippett Studio for its archives; another was sent to Slovakia for reference purposes; the last was given to ILM, where it was cut up into sections and scanned into the computer. The data gathered by such a scan would provide the basis for building the computer model.

In addition to his work in designing Draco, Phil Tippett was also charged with creating computer-generated animatics for the production. Animated video representations of key scenes, animatics would provide the filmmakers with a fully choreographed and far more detailed reference for those scenes than that supplied by static storyboards. "The animatics were a device for Rob and Raffaella to use to collate all the different departments and to block and choreograph some of the action sequences," Tippett explained. "Animatics pull a crew together in a way a storyboard can't, because everybody has his own interpretation of a storyboard. Sometimes it is difficult for actors and crew members to visualize how the scene is going to play out when the computer-animated character is finally put in. That was going to be an even bigger issue on this show, because Rob and Raffaella were going to be dealing with a crew that spoke many different languages. Being able to show these moving pictures really helped to clarify things for them on the set."

Because it would have been cost-prohibitive to produce animatics for every scene in the movie, Tippett and his crew were charged with creating the animation for only one key scene—Bowen's first encounter with Draco and the long fight that follows. "Rob and Raffaella figured that by doing animatics for this one difficult sequence, they would be able to establish parameters that they could rely on for the rest of the production," Tippett explained. Using photographs as reference, the Tippett Studio CG team re-created the Slovakia locations in rough form in the computer. Against those backdrops, two-dimensional representations of Bowen and Draco were rendered and animated to perform all of the actions suggested in the script. Specific camera angles and moves were also incorporated. Within a period of several weeks, the entire fight sequence had been realized in animatic form.

With the completion of the animatics, Phil Tippett's involvement in *Dragonheart* came to an end. All together, the *Dragonheart* assignment had absorbed the studio for nearly eight months. "In some ways," Tippett commented, "*Dragonheart* was an opportunity for me to

improve on the *Dragonslayer* dragon. I'd had ten years to think about that design, and there were things I wanted to do differently. Most of all, I wanted Rob to be happy with his dragon."

Throughout the period during which Cohen was hammering out the design of Draco with Tippett, he was also developing the overall look of the film with Benjamin Fernandez and the art department. To define that look, Cohen began by doing research into the tenth century, an effort that was frustrated by the scarcity of research material available. Paintings from the period provided most of the reference. "We found paintings that had a great deal of detail and told us things such as how they harnessed their horses in the tenth century, how they milled their wheat, what kinds of tools they used," Fernandez said. "Other elements of the design, such as the catapult Bowen uses to slay dragons, were open to imagination and fantasy." Photographs of the *Bayeux tapestry,* one of the few surviving artifacts of the tenth century, were also relied upon for insight and inspiration. Cohen and Fernandez went to great pains to re-create many

"I wanted it to look like no other film."
—Rob Cohen

PRODUCTION

"I wanted to see Draco mythic and glorious in the sun."

—Rob Cohen

By the time Cohen and his crew gathered to begin shooting, the director had already established, in long conversations with director of photography David Eggby, the overall photographic look he wanted for the film. Eggby and Cohen had agreed that the exteriors would be shot in such a way as to suggest a vast and primal landscape. "David and I talked about lighting and how we would shoot the exteriors," Cohen noted. "Within the confines of

the budget we had and the locations we had, we tried to make it look like a beautiful, natural world. We also talked about using wider-angle lenses—I figured if we were going to pay for the whole dragon, we might as well *see* the whole dragon. I thought that the more abstract his image was, the more out of focus, the more unreal he would seem. I also wanted the camera movement to reflect the slower rhythms of the tenth century. I didn't want the movie to be slow, of course, but it had to have a lyric sense of camera movement."

Cohen also wanted the freedom to move his camera at will, without the restrictions that had typically been imposed on movies featuring CG characters. The technical demands of tracking such characters to live-action backgrounds had, until recently, mandated limited camera

movement. Fortunately, CG technology had come a long way by the time *Dragonheart* went into production. "ILM told me I could basically move the camera as much as I wanted," Cohen related, "because they now have the technology to track those camera movements. But they also warned me that tracking is labor-intensive and that it takes a lot of computer time. The more tracking they had to do, the more the shots would cost. So I had to be judicious about how I moved my camera."

Cohen also hoped to fly in the face of traditional effects wisdom by shooting his plates in the brightest sunlight. The vivid, solar look envisioned by the filmmakers had influenced

the choice of locations and the production design, and was equally influential in determining the cinematography style. "Creature movies have always been done in the dark to hide matte lines and wires and rigging," Cohen noted, "but I wanted to *see* this world we were creating. I wanted to see Draco mythic and glorious in the sun. A dragon flying in the sunshine is so much more amazing than a dragon flying against the moon at night. I wanted to see Draco and Bowen walking along in broad daylight, with the dragon just as real in the scene as Bowen's horse. There was a time when it would have been nearly impossible to pull off a CG creature in bright sunshine, but, again, the technology had advanced to the point where it was perfectly feasible."

While the live-action would be shot in standard Panavision, all of the dragon plates would be shot in Vistavision—a larger-format film frame that retains the quality of the image while also allowing maximum flexibility in determining shot composition. "ILM insists on Vistavision—in fact, it is in their contract," said Cohen. "Considering how many Academy Awards they have won for visual effects, I wasn't inclined to argue with them. I saw the value of it, even though it meant having two complete camera systems—Vistavision and the regular Panavision—which was cumbersome. The Vistavision cameras themselves are large and heavy, which makes them difficult to maneuver. But the end result is worth the trouble, because the shots are so breathtakingly clear."

Supervising the Vistavision plate photography was Scott Squires. Support personnel for

the visual effects effort consisted of John Swallow; Mara Hamilton, the visual effects coordinator; and Pat Hadnagy and Brigitte Rasine, both of whom assisted in executing the precise measuring required at each location. Dennis Quaid's brother Buddy was hired originally as a production assistant but was promoted to measurement duty when one of the other crew members left the production. "That was our basic crew for the entire shoot," noted Swallow. "We also had a Vistavision crew which consisted of Robert Stewart and his assistant. It was a fairly small crew, considering the size of the production."

Most of the team's efforts throughout the production revolved around the fact that all of *Dragonheart*'s scenes would be shot without the dragon in attendance. A variety of tools—some high-tech, some simplistic—were employed to ensure that those filmed scenes would provide suitable backgrounds for the insertion of Draco in postproduction. Each shot that would feature the dragon was set up using "monster sticks" of varying heights. Essentially nothing but poles with tennis ball "eyes" on them, the monster sticks gave the actors—usually Dennis Quaid—something to look at in the scene. "Often we used the monster sticks even if the dragon wasn't going to be seen in the shot," Squires explained, "just so the actors would know where to look off-camera. We'd adjust these poles to different heights, depending on Draco's position in the scene. Sometimes he's standing up, sometimes he's lying down, et cetera. We also had some simple full-size mock-up heads—built by Benjamin Fernandez's crew—that we used in some of the scenes for reference."

Another reference tool that was used frequently was the two-and-a-half-foot-long posable dragon model that had been built by the Tippett Studio. "We would pose that model in
front of the camera, calculating what size Draco would be in the frame," Squires commented.
"Then Rob and David Eggby and I would figure out from that what would work best in terms
of placement. We always had to keep Draco's size in mind, whenever we were setting up these
shots. If he was forty-two feet long and eighteen feet tall, we had to make sure that there was

that much room for him in every shot. The actors also had to realize that Draco was there, taking up that amount of space, and they had to learn to work around him."

A vital piece of reference equipment was a microlight airplane that was purchased specifically for the production and was used as a kind of stand-in for the dragon in aerial sequences. Cohen had viewed an IMAX film of the Grand Canyon that had been shot from a microlight, and he determined that the little plane would prove useful during *Dragonheart*'s production.

"The microlight is a little hard-body airplane made in England that holds two people," John Swallow explained. "The plane's wings are about thirty feet across—so it was actually much smaller than Draco, who was supposed to have a wingspan of seventy feet. For the reference shots, the plane would fly into frame and do the moves the dragon was supposedly doing so that the people on the ground could look at it, follow it with their eyes and react to it." The plane would be replaced with the computer-generated dragon in postproduction. To capture aerial footage of Draco's point of view, Swallow and Squires mounted a Vistavision camera on the nose of the microlight. Aerial sequences were supervised by Brian Johnson, an effects veteran and a microlight enthusiast. Piloting the plane was the microlight's designer and builder, David Cook.

"Raffy and I had learned from previous experience that it is best to start a production with the big, killer sequences."
—Rob Cohen

Perhaps the most important piece of equipment employed by the visual effects team was an electronic measuring system that freed the effects crew from the labor- and time-intensive task of measuring large outdoor locations with tape measures. Such measurements would be vital to the CG team when it came time to re-create the on-set environment in the computer and to composite Draco into the shots. "The electronic transit system was crucial," Squires noted. "We were shooting all these large landscapes and there were no man-made structures to use as guides later when we were tracking the camera motion. So we had to take measurements that would provide us with information we needed to track the moves. With the electronic system, we could shoot out an infrared beam toward a target and get our measurements that way. It was a lot faster than having people pull out tape measures."

Despite the efficiency of the electronic measuring system, the *Dragonheart* shoot was a grueling one for the visual effects team. Nine and ten o'clock sunsets enabled Cohen to shoot exceptionally long days; but the visual effects day did not end with the setting of the sun. All of the data gathered during the day's shooting had to be recorded and sent to ILM, where extensive planning of the dragon shots was ongoing. "There was plate information that was really critical on this show because of the dragon," John Swallow remarked. "That information was put into a computer, the computer gave us printouts and all of that material went to ILM."

ILM was also kept up-to-date throughout the shoot by an Internet link set up by Squires. "I took my PowerBook with me and went over to the phone at the hotel every night.

That way I could keep in touch with the people at ILM. We were on a different timeline, and regular phone bills would have been astronomical. This way we could give ILM updates every day, and I could get feedback even if I came on at odd hours."

The Internet would serve as Squires's lifeline as he and his fellow crew members met the day-in, day-out challenges of the four-and-a-half-month shoot.

The first scene slated for filming was one in which Bowen attempts to light a campfire on the ledge of a cliff, with Draco in attendance. Cohen and his crew had found an ideal location for the scene—a rising cliff in Slovakia's scenic national forest, outside the town of Levoca. Although the forest belonged to the Slovakian army, the filmmakers had little difficulty in securing the location. "One of the great things about working in Slovakia," Cohen noted, "was that there wasn't a real strong government, so there wasn't a lot of bureaucratic nonsense to plow through. It was very easy

"That first day, I was thinking to myself, 'Oh, my God, this is going to be miserable . . . and I've got five months to go.'"
—Dennis Quaid

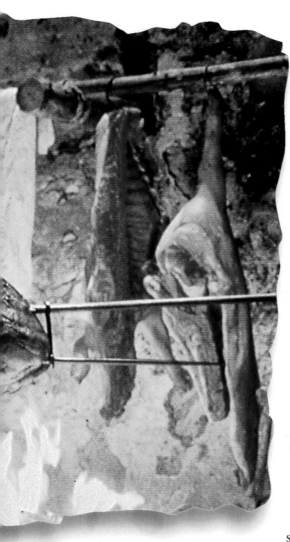

to maneuver around the country. When we found out this endless forest belonged to the army, it was a simple matter to negotiate with them and get permission to shoot there. To try to shoot in a national forest in the United States would have been a *major* headache. Milan Stanisic, our production manager, and his crew were all Croatian, so they knew their way around. They managed to cut through the red tape very quickly."

Cast and crew were transported near the precipitous location—which featured a five-hundred-foot drop—but had to hike the final three-quarters of a mile to the top. "That day was hard," Dennis Quaid recalled. "We got the wrong directions to the set, so we were an hour late. Then, one of the stuntmen that was going to double for me fell off a cart on the way up and broke his wrist. When we finally got there, we were on this huge cliff and it was windy and we were trying to get the campfire going just right. That first day, I was thinking to myself, 'Oh, my God, this is going to be miserable . . . and I've got five months to go.'"

The first day of filming was also somewhat rocky for the director. "I was very nervous," Cohen admitted. "Not only was it the start of filming, but I could just see someone making a false move and going over that ledge. I was also nervous because it was the first time I would see Dennis interacting with Draco—who, of course, wasn't there. Dennis had the thankless job of carrying not only his own role, but the dragon's. As we started, I had some trepidation about how he would pull that off. But as soon as we began filming, I relaxed. Dennis was there in that black tenth-century outfit, throwing looks toward Draco, and I saw life coming out, as if the dragon was real for him. From the time we shot that first scene, I knew I was in the right place at the right time with the right people."

The campfire scene was only the first of many in which Quaid would be required to play a scene with Draco without benefit of the dragon's appearance. "The relationship between Bowen and Draco reminded me a little of the relationship I had with the creature in *Enemy Mine*," Quaid said. "The big difference was that, in that movie, the character was actually *there*—there was an actor underneath the lizard suit. This was very different because I was acting with air, so it was much more of a challenge to create a relationship. There was an upside to it, too: I never had to worry about my costar's behavior; he was always on time; I never had to wait for him; he never missed a cue. I've been acting in movies for twenty years now, so I was able to just look at this as one more thing I had to deal with for this particular shoot."

For Quaid, envisioning the dragon in a scene was an internal exercise. "One of the things I did to make Draco real for me was that I played to the dragon within myself. In the Western world, the dragon is a symbol for the wild, untamed parts of ourselves—and we all have that. To do a scene with Draco, I played to that part of myself that is not civilized."

Although Quaid's acting skill would be relied upon to provide most of the interaction between knight and dragon in the campfire scene, a moment in which Draco bends to shout into Bowen's face required the implementation of air hoses to create the illusion of the dragon's breath blowing the knight's hair. In one take, Rob Cohen manned the air hoses himself to get just the look he was after.

As dusk gives way to night, the scene continues with Draco suddenly falling back in pain—the result of a wound inflicted on Einon by Kara. It is the first hint in the movie of the Corsican Brother–like connection between Einon and the dragon. In part because of the inherent danger of shooting at night on the cliff, the scene was filmed five miles down the road on a matching ledge built and erected a safe four feet off the ground by Benjamin Fernandez and his crew. At that location, Kit West's team rigged trees to fall as Draco collapsed in pain. Also required was a full-size section of Draco's wounded shoulder built by ILM, for a shot in which Bowen lays a blanket over his suffering friend.

The same mock-up ledge served as the location for an earlier scene between Bowen and Gilbert in which Bowen scoffs at the monk's quest to find Avalon. "It was the magic hour," Rob Cohen

recalled, "and we had the joy of watching Pete Postlethwaite work for the first time. He was, right from the start, right on the money with this character. He was funny and touching and brilliant. He did a deft comedic turn, at the same time creating a very poignant performance."

With the shooting of the campfire scenes, the production got off to a relatively uneventful start. The next few days would be spent shooting the far more demanding tor sequence. The castle situated close to Spisska had been modified by Benjamin Fernandez and the construction crew to facilitate the needs of the production; even so, filming at the site was a laborious task. "It was a huge ruin of a castle," Cohen related, "so lighting it was very difficult. We also had rain towers set up everywhere because it was supposed to be a rainy scene. Logistically, it was a very difficult few days. Raffy and I had learned from previous experience that it is best to start a production with the big, killer sequences. Everybody is fresh and enthusiastic at the beginning, and doing the hard stuff puts everything immediately into high gear."

The only disadvantage to shooting the tor section so early in the schedule was that it forced Dennis Quaid into some of his most pivotal scenes. It is

here, in Avalon, that Bowen has the epiphany that will lead him to join the peasant rebels in their fight against Einon. "It was a tough thing to throw Dennis into so early," de Laurentiis admitted, "but he was absolutely great. We started with the scene at the end of the second act, the moment where Draco has told him that he is the dragon that gave the heart to Einon. It is a turning point for Bowen, the point at which he realizes that he has been wrong about Einon all along. Dennis played the scene beautifully; and as I watched it on the monitor, I knew we had the right Bowen."

Quaid himself considered the early scheduling of the tor scenes to be advantageous. "I'm

glad we went there so early," he said, "because it allowed me to jump right into the thick of things. At the tor, things really started to gel. There were many complicated shots that had to be coordinated with the different departments, but they all came together. It was at the tor that I relaxed and realized that we were going to make a movie."

Dialogue scenes between Bowen and Draco had, up to this point, been executed with either a recording of Sean Connery's performance being turned on and off at the appropriate moments or with an actor hired specifically for the purpose of speaking Draco's lines from off-camera. The recording had been arranged before the beginning of the shoot, with Cohen and Quaid flying to Nassau to meet with Connery. A two-day session in a studio resulted in a complete recording of Draco's dialogue. That recording would not only serve as performance reference for Quaid and Cohen on the set, it was also vital to budgeting the visual effects shots, since Connery's line readings would be the determining factor in how long each dragon shot was going to be.

By the time the shoot began, Cohen had already spent innumerable hours editing the recording; as a result, the director was intimately familiar with all the nuances of Connery's performance. At the tor, Cohen took over the job of playing Draco from off-camera, reading the dragon's lines over the production PA system. It was a practice he would continue throughout the shoot. "I had heard this recording and worked with it over and over again, so I had a pretty good idea of how Sean had delivered each line," Cohen said. "So when the actor we hired to do Draco's lines didn't work out, I said, 'Just give me the mike,' and I started doing it myself. At the end of that night, Dennis came to me and said, 'Could you keep doing that for me? You give it some feeling, and that helps me.' So I started to play Draco, reading the lines as closely as I could to the way Sean had read them."

"During the shoot," Quaid said, "Rob actually *became* Draco to me. He didn't just read the lines, he acted them. I was able to develop a relationship with Draco because Rob was so fantastic in the part. Through Rob, the dragon was actually there for me." With mike in hand throughout a large part of the shoot, Cohen took to using the PA system as a tool to expedite his directing duties. "I started getting lazy," he said laughing. "I'd use the PA system to direct, which, understandably, annoyed David Eggby. I'd say, 'NO, PAN THE CAMERA TO THE LEFT' on mike. It was really convenient to do it that way, because these locations were huge."

Shooting continued at the tor, with the first unit filming live-action scenes within the castle courtyard and the visual effects crew concentrating its efforts on Draco's airborne

approach of Avalon. Having just rescued Bowen, Gilbert and Kara from a mob of angry villagers, Draco carries the trio—and the horse upon which they are perched—in his claw as he flies toward the legendary castle. From his POV, the misty clouds part and Avalon is revealed below. The moment when Avalon is revealed was shot from the microlight plane and was enhanced in postproduction with matte paintings rendered by Illusion Arts.

Shortly afterward, Draco, Kara and Gilbert depart Avalon, intent on organizing an army to bring down King Einon. Alone and in despair, Bowen begins to hear the voices of King Arthur and the knights of the round table. As he enters the graveyard to investigate, a beam of light radiates from the main pillar, revealing Arthur's face. For the shot, Fernandez's crew modeled a stone column into which a likeness of King Arthur—John Gielgud—was sculpted on one side. Set up on a turntable, the stone column was photographed, then rotated to facilitate filming of the sculpted features.

Draco then returns, approaching his friend Bowen and extending his wing to protect him from the rain. An attempt was made to rig a canvas panel in the approximate size and shape of Draco's wing that could be moved over Quaid's body, thus simulating Draco's protective gesture. But on each take, the canvas would fill with water before the move across Quaid was completed, causing it to sag with the extra weight. More than once, the actor had to duck to avoid being hit by the low-hanging, water-filled canvas. After two tries, the practical approach was scrapped and the decision was made to leave the "rain removal" to the digital artists in postproduction.

From the tor, the company moved to the Felton's mill set, situated near the town of Martin. "Martin was a communist showcase town," Dennis Quaid revealed. "Instead of grass

"It was 110 degrees on some days, and people were being stung by toxic yellow jackets and rushed to the hospital for adrenaline shots."
—Rob Cohen

on the lawns, there was broken glass. The buildings were gray. It was a factory town with a river that was polluted. It was very depressing—but then, when we got the set, we really felt as if we were in the tenth century."

"Then this extraordinary explosion went off and all the extras started running as fast as they could. That wasn't good acting on their parts—that was real terror." —Scott Squires

Here, Draco and Bowen pull off their first scam at the expense of Felton, one of Einon's henchmen who, like his king, is in the process of building a stone castle. Sets at the location included the castle-in-progress and surrounding grain mills. "There was a lot involved in the Felton's mill sequence," Cohen said. "There were huge fire effects, plus we were dealing for the first time with peasants, horses and a lot of tenth-century trappings. It was a big deal for us." As scripted, Bowen's scam at Felton's mill would begin with Draco flying over the site, then firing off a series of fireballs that result in the disintegration of the mill. Kit

West rigged an elaborate setup to create the fiery explosions. "Rob wanted it to look like a Vietnam War napalm attack," West explained, "where the fire would come down and the whole area would catch alight. Major construction was required to pull that off. We had to lay down something like a quarter mile of gasoline-filled plastic pipes. Alongside those pipes we had gunpowder and flash charges which ignited the gasoline. We started the charge at one end and ran it across the entire area."

Four cameras—three Vistavision cameras and one four-perf camera—were set up at Felton's mill to capture the explosion and provide the background plate into which a flying, dive-bombing Draco would be composited. "We had estimated that the fire was going to go up about forty feet," Squires recalled, "so we framed everything with that in mind. But when the explosion went off, the flames went up about a hundred and twenty feet. It was phenomenal. Right before we shot this, Rob had said to Kit, 'Is this going to burn the flesh off of me?' He was standing about a quarter mile from the fire, and Kit had said, 'Oh, no, you

might feel a little bit of heat, but that's all.' Then this extraordinary explosion went off and all the extras started running as fast as they could. That wasn't good acting on their parts—that was real terror."

Although the oversized explosion made for spectacular footage, it significantly complicated the addition of Draco flying overhead, since flames and smoke now consumed the area of the sky where the dragon was supposed to be positioned. To create the interaction of Draco flying through the attendant smoke of the explosion—and to give the running extras something to react to in the sky—the microlight plane was flown over the location as the explosions were set off. "The microlight flew right through the smoke," Squires explained. "The idea was that the wings of the plane would create a vortexing effect that we could use to suggest Draco's wings were flying through. But the plane didn't really give us much in the way of interactive swirling in the smoke, so we knew we were going to have to go in and add some CG elements to create that effect later on."

His mill destroyed and his castle threatened, Felton is more than willing to pay Bowen to slay the menacing dragon. Setting up his "whacker"—a catapult device designed and built by the art department—Bowen aims a giant arrow toward the dragon flying overhead. As planned, Draco catches the arrow in the pit of his wing, then launches into overly dramatic death throes, finally plummeting into a body of water below. To indicate Draco's fall into the water, an interactive splash was created by dropping three fifty-five-gallon drums, welded together, from a helicopter hovering over a lake on location.

For a subsequent shot following Draco as he swims underwater, plates were photographed from a crane stationed on a ferryboat moving across the lake. One of the full-size heads built by the art department was filmed specifically for the purpose of extracting water highlights that would be glinting off the dragon's head as it rises from the water. Additional shots of water splashing and

dripping were photographed by the second unit later in the schedule to provide ILM with a variety of water elements to use in conjunction with its CG character.

Following the triumph at Felton's mill, Bowen is revealed walking through a grassy landscape in a long tracking camera move, with Draco flying overhead. The elaborate setup on location included 120 feet of track laid up the side of a very steep, grassy hill, and a counterweighted dolly system that enabled the crew to move the camera smoothly up the incline without benefit of a motorized rig. To ensure that Dennis Quaid looked at the appropriate spots in the sky during his exchange of dialogue with Draco, Buddy Quaid ran alongside the actor and his horse, holding a long pole for eye-line reference. "We couldn't use the microlight for this scene," Squires explained, "because Draco was supposed to be circling Bowen, and the radius was too tight for the plane to manage. It was also too dangerous to come in that low to Dennis."

The scene also required practical effects to create the movement of the grass as Draco lands and walks beside Bowen in the tall vegetation. Initially, West's crew employed small toboggans which were dragged through the field to make the grass depress in a footprint pattern. Toboggans were also used to create the interactive effect of the tail dragging through the grass. When the technique proved awkward and produced less than satisfactory results, someone suggested that the foot and tail impressions could be made more efficiently by having crew members lie on their backs and create grassy versions of snow angels. "Coming from England, I'd never heard of snow angels," West said. "When the idea was first suggested, I didn't know what everybody was talking about! But then the crew got down on the ground and demonstrated. It was a great idea, and it worked beautifully."

Scenes in a wheat field and swamp village were shot nearby. "We found the ideal place for the wheat field," Benjamin Fernandez noted. "It was a golden field with mountains in the background and forest surrounding it. It was just perfect. The contrast of the colors and textures made for an astonishing location."

"We did sixteen nights in below-zero weather, on top of this mountain, in a drafty old castle. We thought we were going to die."
—Raffaella de Laurentiis

"Our wheat field looked like European wheat of the period rather than pristine, herbicide-treated American wheat," Cohen added. "In the Middle Ages and earlier, wheat grew among other grasses and weeds, and it never grew very high. I wanted a location that would reflect that, and luckily we found one."

In the wheat field, Bowen gives chase to an old dragon—dubbed "the old scarred one"—and meets up with Gilbert for the first time. Although the old scarred one is never actually revealed in the scene, her presence is suggested in a shadow moving across Gilbert and in the whipping of the wheat as the dragon flies low. "This scene was fairly early in the movie," Rob Cohen said, "before we'd seen Draco in all his glory. I didn't want to blow Draco's big entrance by showing another dragon first, so we decided to shoot this scene in such a way that the old dragon would be suggested, but not seen. Also, the sequence wasn't important enough to justify spending a lot of money to do CG dragon shots. By shooting the scene with the dragon as just an oblique presence, I was able to retain Draco's mystery *and* save money."

*"I've worked in
Mexico, in mainland China,
all over Europe
—but I've never had as good
an experience as I did
in Eastern Europe."*
—Raffaella de Laurentiis

While the shadow would be created as a relatively simple, low-cost CG effect, the movement of the wheat as the dragon flies overhead was achieved practically with large, powerful Ritter fans stationed just outside of frame. "It took a lot of careful timing and synchronization to get the wheat to move in just the right way," West said. "We had to coordinate our fans and the moving wheat so that they would match up with Gilbert following the flight of the dragon with his eyes."

From the wheat field, the company moved to the swamp village set built by Benjamin Fernandez and his team on a dammed river near the Hungarian border. The site of a scene in which Bowen and Draco's scam goes awry, the swamp village featured crude huts situated on a swampy island, connected to the mainland through a series of wooden bridges. "I liked that location very much, because the landscape was so interesting," Fernandez commented.

"There were so many pigs there, we tripped over them."
—Dina Meyer

Scenes at the swamp village required dozens of extras to play peasants; and, in fact, Rob Cohen himself dirtied his face and donned the tattered garb of a villager. The swamp village was also populated by more than a hundred pigs, imported from Hungary. "There were so many pigs there," Dina Meyer recalled, "we tripped over them. We'd be shooting a scene and these pigs would be grunting in the background, chomping on their food. It was distracting—and *funny*! This was supposed to be a very serious scene for Kara, but it was all I could do not to laugh through the whole thing because of these pigs."

At the swamp, Draco is to make another bogus death plunge and swim away. But after diving with great theatrics into the water, he discovers that it is too shallow for swimming, and the dragon's massive body is momentarily stuck in the mud. As peasants gather at water's edge, it appears that the game is up.

The scene required Kit West to devise a means to suggest that a creature of Draco's size and weight had fallen into the swampy pond. "The way it was storyboarded," West said, "Draco was to hit the mud with his head first and then his body was to fall backward, knocking down trees as it fell. Of course, on location we had trees and we had water, but no Draco. So we had to create the splashes— a splash for when his head hits, and then a series of splashes as his body falls. At the same time, we had to make the trees part. We built synthetic trees and put them on trips and spring mechanisms so they would fall in a series, like a domino effect. Then, to get the splashes, we dropped weights from a helicopter."

Unfortunately, windy conditions made it nearly impossible for the helicopter to maneuver, and the weights repeatedly landed off-target. In addition, the spring-loaded trees were too light and thus did not fall with an appropriate sense of mass. During postproduction, long after filming had been completed, the decision was made to return to the site and reshoot the sequence. "We went back and set up larger trees," said John Swallow. "They were rigged to bungee cords that would

release them at the press of a trigger. We also brought a hundred-twenty-foot crane in to drop weights for the splash. With the crane we were able to pinpoint the target more accurately, without having to worry about a helicopter holding steady. For a second shot, a side view, we put a big tube which had a ring around it in the water. We released the ring so that it would come down and create another splash, and then the tube itself fell over, representing Draco's body. The crew released the trees as this tube fell. Kit put the whole thing together in a couple of weeks, and the reshoot itself only took a couple of days. This scene was the only thing we had to redo, which was pretty amazing."

Filmed on location during principal photography were background plates for subsequent shots of Draco stuck in the mud. Simple, full-size prop pieces painted black were provided by the art department and filmed to represent the dragon's arms and neck sticking out of the water. "We put mud and water all over those props, just to give us an idea of how that should look when we replaced those pieces with the CG Draco," Squires said. "We also had some crew people wrapped in black moving in the water to create more interaction—each person represented a foot or an arm on Draco."

The swamp villagers, angry with the knowledge that they have been duped by Bowen and Draco, advance on the mud-encased dragon. Draco struggles free of the mud and runs downriver, away from the mob, finally lifting off into the air. The background plates for the scene required a long dolly move past the swamp village huts and the running villagers in the foreground. Splash elements were also filmed to suggest Draco's scrambling feet in the water as he makes his escape.

In the following scene, Draco swoops down to rescue Bowen, Gilbert and Kara, who are attempting their own escape on horseback. Surrounded by the angry mob, the three protagonists and their mount are suddenly scooped up by the dragon and flown to safety. A plate was shot of Quaid, Meyer and Postlethwaite on horseback, surrounded by villagers. Then, a sec-

ond plate was shot with only the villagers in the scene. In postproduction, a transition between the two plates would be achieved with Draco's computer generated wing entering, then exiting the frame.

As the schedule moved into late summer, filming continued in the forests surrounding Bratislava. Here, the waterfall and cave where Bowen meets with Draco were built by Fernandez's crew and engineered for real running water by Kit West. The same waterfall set would be employed for a later scene in which Kara, Draco and Bowen are confronted by Einon and his men.

Europe had fallen into the grip of a record-breaking heat wave just as the waterfall exterior shoot began. "We really suffered during the filming of the waterfall scenes," Cohen said. "It was 110 degrees on some days, and people were being stung by toxic yellow jackets and rushed to the hospital for adrenaline shots. There was the smell of chlorine from the water, which wasn't pleasant. Kit and his guys couldn't change millions of gallons of water every day, so by the end of a few days the water would be filthy and filled with horse manure. It was miserable for everybody."

It was particularly miserable for Dennis Quaid, who was on a skittish horse throughout most of the waterfall scenes. "The horse kept throwing me," Quaid said with a laugh, "but I couldn't really blame him. The horse was shoulder-deep in water, and he had a guy on his back wearing eighty pounds of armor. There was a camera in front of him and all these people. He'd be fine until someone said, 'Rolling'—and then he'd flip out. I think the sound of the camera must have bothered him. It would take me three or four takes to get him to do what we had rehearsed.

"The other problem was that, in this scene, Draco is throwing out pieces of dead knights. So things were being thrown toward the horse. On the first take, a piece of armor came flying out—and the horse went crazy. The next thing I knew, I was underwater. It was pretty scary. But I felt very protected throughout the shoot. I was very well taken care of, in terms of safety. On any shoot, what the actors go through is nothing compared to what the crew goes through."

The site of this unpleasant few days of shooting was an abandoned quarry. Synthetic rocks surrounding the waterfall and the cave behind it were carved and painted to match the real rock faces. "We had to carve into the real rock that was there and cover it with plaster," Fernandez explained. "Because the dimensions of the cave were so big—about three hundred feet long by thirty-six feet high—we had to weld together a steel structure to support it."

The waterfall itself was approximately thirty-five feet tall and twenty feet wide. "The waterfall fell into a stream, which we created as well," explained Kit West. "We dug a trench that was about two-and-a-half-feet deep and then lined it with waterproof material. The water came over the waterfall, ran into this stream and then was recirculated and pumped back up to the top. We had some-

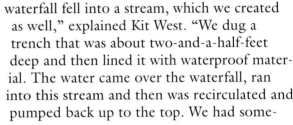

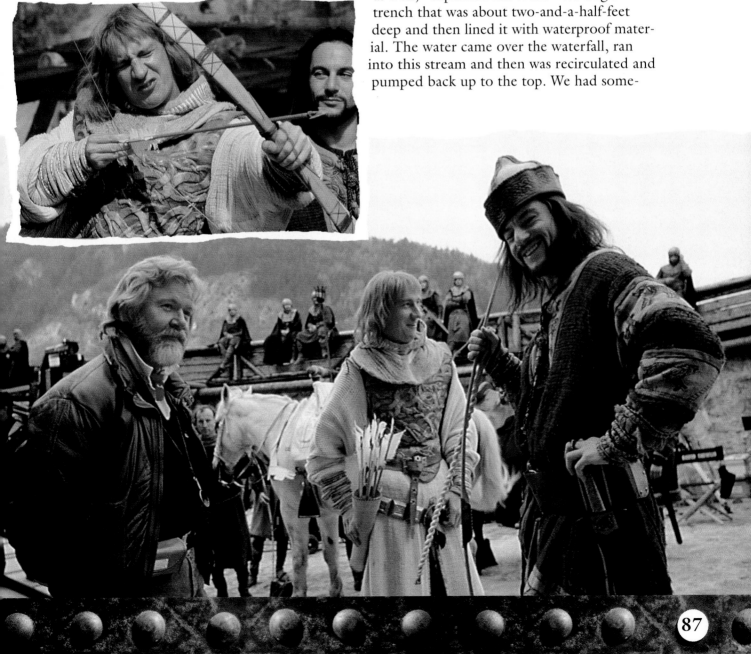

thing like twenty-five submersible pumps pumping several hundred thousand gallons of water continuously."

The first waterfall scene begins with Gilbert coming to rest on what looks like a giant rock. When the "rock" opens its eye, the friar is thrown off his perch, and the dragon quickly retreats to the cave behind the waterfall. A piece of Styrofoam carved and painted to resemble Draco's head was raised for the shot of Gilbert tumbling from his seat. In the following shot,

Draco's tail is seen exiting behind the waterfall. Although a CG tail would eventually be put into the scene, a large metal cone that was similar in shape to the dragon's tail was filmed to capture the appropriate interaction between tail and water. "The cone was on a rig inside the cave, and they would move it back and forth on a dolly," Squires explained. "We had a couple of different cameras set up, and we shot both clean waterfall plates and this interactive footage with the cone."

After being discovered by Bowen, Draco bursts out from behind the waterfall and takes flight. To create the effect of Draco's body launching out from behind the wall of water, Kit West's crew set off a series of mortars. "Our first view of Draco coming through the falls is from the side," explained John Swallow. "We see his head, then his shoulders break through.

Kit timed that out so that the mortars went off, boom, boom, boom, as if Draco's body was blasting through the waterfall." Aiding in the timing of the effect were the animatics produced by the Tippett Studio. "We could see on the animatic what the timing needed to be. It took several takes, because all we had were guys on triggers, setting off these mortars. There was a lot of room for error." Computer-generated effects would reveal Draco flying toward camera and then rising above the frame as the camera tilts up. A CG shadow falling across Gilbert would also be added in postproduction.

In the story, Draco, Bowen and Kara return to the waterfall after Kara's fellow villagers have offered her up as a sacrifice to the dragon. The shooting of the scene represented Dina Meyer's first one-on-one interaction with the invisible Draco. "Shooting that scene was one of the toughest experiences for me," Meyer recalled. "They had these markers up—orange balls on tall sticks—and they said, 'This is where Draco is going to be.' Then they took the markers away for the filming, so I had to focus on a tree branch or anything stationary I could find to mark Draco's position in my mind. What made it more difficult was that Draco was going to be moving as he spoke his lines, so I had to follow him with my eyes. Rob would say, 'He'll be here on this line and there on this line,' and I would have to memorize all of that and keep it in mind while I was talking to this imaginary character. On top of that, I was trying to remember my lines and thinking about where the camera was and trying to act—all at the same time."

Equally challenging was the filming of Einon's approach and his long sword battle with Bowen at the waterfall. Not only was the fight scene one of the most demanding of the film, it also marked David Thewlis's first day of work on *Dragonheart*. "Dennis and I had never actually fought together," Thewlis recalled. "We'd been working with wooden swords, on dry land, with stuntmen. Suddenly we were in the water with real swords, in full costume on a baking hot day—and I didn't know what the hell I was doing. I was rather bewildered, because I'd never done anything like it in my life.

I was very scared, and yet determined to get it right. I think it took two days to film the sword fight, and at the end of the second day I felt such a sense of achievement. 'Yes! I did it!'"

The forest environs outside Bratislava also served as the site for Kara's village, where the production moved at the end of the summer to film the initial battle scene in which young Einon is wounded, the second scam sequence and, finally, the war camp and training scenes that occur

"It was a big Robin Hood type of battle, with arrows flying and people being caught on fire."
—Kit West

near the film's climax. A small clearing in the forest had been uncovered during the location scout and was an ideal spot for the setting of Kara's village. "There was a little stream there," Fernandez said, "so I decided to build a bridge and a little dam to create a pond under the bridge. It made sense in terms of the story, because it would create a bit of protection for the village. When we were finished shooting, we returned the land to its original condition."

We first see the village in turmoil, as the young girl Kara witnesses the slaughter of her people by Einon's father, King Freyne. The opening battle at Kara's village was a huge practical effects sequence orchestrated by Kit West. "It was a big Robin Hood type of battle," said West, "with arrows flying and people being caught on fire. At the end of it, King Freyne's men torch

all the huts, which was another big fire sequence we had to work out."

Fourteen years later, Bowen returns with Draco to Kara's village. As in the Felton's mill sequence, Draco is seen flying over the village, terrorizing the peasants—a scene for which background POV plates were made by mounting the Vistavision camera on the microlight. In the course of his attack, Draco also shears the roof off one of the huts, shattering it with his tail. On the set, the targeted hut was rigged by West so that a section of its thatched roof would self-destruct on cue.

Also lensed at the site was the scene in which Kara is put onto a cart and offered up as a sacrifice to the dragon. It appears that the villagers' sacrifice is accepted when Draco swoops down and plucks both Kara and the cart from the ground. The scene was photographed once with Dina Meyer in the stationary cart, and a second time with an empty cart that was lifted with wires. Those two separate plates were split in postproduction and combined to make it appear as if Kara was in the cart as it was lifted.

Within the context of the story, Kara, Draco and Bowen return to Kara's village to organize a peasant rebellion after Bowen's epiphany at the tor. Captured on film was a scene in which Bowen rides up a ridge and signals for Draco's appearance. The following shot of Draco rising up dramatically behind him, in silhouette against a blazing sun, would be created as a visual effect in postproduction. A montage revealing the peasants in various stages of training were the last shots filmed at the location.

The montage comes to an end with the discovery of the encampment by Brok, one of Einon's men. Draco, drinking from a pond, looks up to see the man, and emits a bellowing roar. For the background plate, a crew member was tasked with moving the water in the pond as if Draco were drinking. The most troublesome aspect of the shot were the ducks swimming peacefully in the water. "In every take, the ducks insisted on swimming over to the area where Draco's head was supposed to be," recalled Squires. "The other problem was that the ducks should have reacted if Draco was really there roaring—but they didn't flinch, of course, since there was no Draco and no roaring." There was no choice but to resort to "digital duck removal" in postproduction, implementing the same digital techniques commonly used to remove wires and cables in effects films. The unwanted elements—in this case, ducks—would be painted out and replaced with the more appropriate surrounding imagery.

> *"What we put this poor guy through! Dennis was in a harness, being flown all over the forest for days!"*
> —Raffaella de Laurentiis

No scenes filmed at the forest location were more complicated or demanding than the extended fight between Draco and Bowen that takes place after Draco has burst from the waterfall to escape the dragonslayer. Hot in pursuit, Bowen captures the airborne dragon's leg with one of his bolos and is subsequently flown through the forest.

Kit West's crew rigged up the harness and wire apparatus that would enable them to fly Dennis Quaid through the wooded location. "There were some quite tricky movements in that sequence," West noted. "It wasn't straight Peter Pan–style flying—he was hitting trees and bouncing all over the place, so we had to use pretty sub-

stantial cables. For some shots we had cranes overhead that the wires were attached to. In other cases, the wires were strung across two forty-foot towers. Dennis Quaid was in a harness, holding on to a kind of leather whip, and we flew him either from the crane or from one tower to another."

Quaid did the vast majority of the flying stunt work himself. "What we put this poor guy through," de Laurentiis moaned. "Dennis was in a harness, being flown all over the forest for days! He was a real trooper."

"I actually thought the flying was fun," Quaid said. "It was a good ride. Kit rigged the harness so it was fairly comfortable—which was a good thing, because I was suspended in it sometimes for a couple of hours at a time. It was too much trouble to keep getting in and out

of the harness, so I'd stay in it for long periods of time. But it wasn't bad at all. It was a little like floating in water. I'd close my eyes and relax and try to forget that I was in Slovakia."

After being dragged through the forest, Bowen finally manages to wrestle the dragon to the ground. The dust and debris that kick up as Draco falls were realized as practical effects. "We shot that a couple of times," West recalled. "The first time we did it, it was too much—it looked like a big explosion. So we redid that shot using air mortars to get the right amount of dust coming up." Also filmed on the spot, via a crane move, was Gilbert running up a hillside to watch Bowen's battle with the dragon in the gully below.

To ensure that Quaid's actions and reactions would make sense when the CG dragon was composited into the scene, the entire fight sequence had to be choreographed precisely. The timing of actions such as the dragon's tail hitting the ground and

trees was particularly painstaking. While most of the tail shots in the fight would be computer-generated, a full-scale urethane and fiberglass prop, built by the ILM creature shop, was used for a shot of Draco's tail hitting Bowen squarely in the chest, knocking the knight to the ground.

ILM also built a life-size claw employed for a shot of the dragon pinning Bowen beneath his foot. The spring-loaded claw was bolted into the ground with Quaid beneath it. Lifelike movement was simulated by crew members manually manipulating the claw from off-camera. "It was particularly difficult to make those full-size pieces work," Squires commented, "because they were going to be inserted between all of the CG elements. In direct comparison, those kinds of foam or urethane devices don't hold up as well as they might by themselves. It was a cost-saving measure to use full-size pieces for a few shots, but we couldn't use them in too many shots, or let the camera hold on them for too long."

The long battle between Bowen and Draco eventually deteriorates into an even longer standoff, with the knight inside the dragon's mouth. There, Bowen aims his sword at Draco's soft palate so that if the dragon bites down, the sword will pierce his brain. Conversely, if the knight stabs the dragon, the mouth will close and Bowen will be crushed between the creature's massive teeth. With both adversaries thus in check, the standoff continues throughout the night.

From the beginning of the storyboarding phase, Cohen's intention had been to shoot the scene almost entirely from inside the dragon's mouth. "I wanted to shoot it as if the camera was right behind the uvula," Cohen explained. "I wanted the audience to feel what it would be like to be inside a dragon's mouth—this disgusting, living cave with spit and bad breath."

To facilitate Cohen's idea, the ILM creature shop built a full-size mechanical tongue and jaw rig that was puppeteered on location. A CG Draco head would be wrapped around the animatronic jaws in postproduction to complete the illusion. Construction of the animatronic tongue and jaw was headed up by Jeff Olson, Mike Steffe and Eben Stromquist, while creature shop supervisor Jean Bolte coordinated the effort and acted as liaison with Kit West, who would provide a support rig upon which the animatronic head would be mounted.

The construction of the dragon's mouth began with drawings that were scaled up to the appropriate size. "We projected the drawings, putting one of our sculptors, Richard Miller, next to the projection and drawing around him to make sure it would be big enough for Dennis Quaid to stand inside," Olson explained. "We photographed that and sent it to Rob and Raffaella so they could evaluate it. We did that back and forth a few times. When we were certain that we had the size right, we then built a three-dimensional mock-up out of

plywood and foam, with carved foam teeth."

The mock-up was approved by Cohen during one of his preproduction visits to ILM, and the creature shop subsequently began working out the mechanics that would be necessary to articulate the mouth and tongue. "We did numerous mock-ups and design models to make sure that the mechanics would fit inside the rig and that the overall rig would fit atop Kit West's support structure," said Olson. "Finally, we had everything ready to begin building the real mouth and tongue." In the final version, the gums and upper palate were made of a hard-cast plastic, supported by an aluminum frame. "The teeth were made of semihard materials so that if someone accidentally whacked himself on one of the teeth, it would give a little bit. The teeth couldn't be so soft that they would bend and flex, but we had to keep safety in mind."

The tongue was made of urethane-coated foam and was mechanized to perform a number of realistic tongue movements. "We spent most of our engineering time making sure the tongue would move convincingly," Olson recalled. "It was quite a challenge, because the tongue was going to be visible while the dragon was speaking, so it had to be able to move with a lot of

agility and flexibility. We finally came up with a hydraulic mechanism that enabled it to shift in and out of the mouth, as well as curl, twist and flatten out."

The creature shop team traveled to Slovakia in September to puppeteer the animatronic device for the standoff scene. Originally slated to stay for only a week, the team's stay was extended to six weeks when mechanical difficulties involving the Vistavision cameras had to be ironed out. Once on-site, the tongue—enhanced with liver spots and drool applied by the production makeup artists—performed flawlessly.

"The tongue was absolutely lifelike," Cohen observed. "When they first fired up the hydraulics and the tongue started to move, I looked at it and thought, 'My God, that is eerie.' That tongue could do everything a human tongue could do. It was a great achievement."

Slowly, the heat of summer was giving way to the cooler temperatures of autumn. The shift in the air foretold a harsh Eastern European winter, during which time the production would have no choice but to retreat to the indoor stages in Bratislava. Fortunately, all that remained before the move to the studio were three weeks of filming at Einon's castle in Zilina, in the eastern part of the country. "We finished our location work at Einon's castle because it was at least somewhat contained," explained Raffaella de Laurentiis. "We didn't want to be out in a field somewhere that near to wintertime, where we would have been stuck if a snowstorm started. The castle was old and drafty, but at least there were stone walls. We still froze our butts, though. We did sixteen nights in below-zero weather, on top of this mountain, in a drafty old castle. We thought we were going to die. But it worked for the film. You could see all this breath coming out as people talked, and that added to the dramatic quality of the ending."

The site of Draco's death scene and the peasant uprising against Einon, the castle—situated on a steep rock face two hundred feet in the air—had been discovered during the first four-day scout in Slovakia. Local legend had it that the castle had once been run by a woman who regularly tortured young girls to death and then bathed in their blood in an attempt to stay young. "Slovakia was full of stories like that," Cohen noted. "We heard many legends about people of power torturing others just for the fun of it."

Despite its colorful ambiance, the castle required extensive construction before it perfectly suited the production's requirements. Built in the tenth century, all that remained of the castle's origins were the foundations. Repeated renovations through the centuries had resulted in a mishmash of styles throughout the structure. As recently as the Second World War, the castle had been completely demolished and rebuilt once again. "In the rebuilding," Fernandez commented, "they had added things from different periods, including modern structures, so we had to modify it to look as if it was built in the tenth century. We built columns and put in

the right kinds of archways. The windows were also too big and were out of the time period, so we built fake windows and added them to the existing window frames. The tower where Bowen and Einon fight at the end was also built from scratch." Interior sets such as the banquet room and Kara's prison were incorporated into rooms in the castle, with appropriate doors, windows and stairways added as needed. "It was helpful that, in the story, Einon was

supposed to be in the process of building this castle, so it didn't have to look as if it was completely finished. We were able to leave scaffolding and things like that all over it."

Renovations were completed by the time the company arrived at the location to shoot the large-scale battle between Bowen's peasant rebels and Einon's army. An initial attack shot reveals Draco swooping down on a line of archers at the top of the castle wall, shooting flames and creating a wall of fire that prompts the archers to jump from the top of the fortress to their deaths below. Stuntmen were positioned at the top of a castle wall and were instructed to fall as the practical flame effects were initiated. When the huge fireball explosion went off early, some of the stuntmen were caught in the flames before they'd had a chance to jump. Fortunately, all were wearing fireproof, protective garments and no one was seriously hurt. More distant explosions—featured in long shots of Draco firing on the castle—would be added as CG elements in postproduction.

Joining the melee are dragonslayers hired by Aislinn, who has come to understand that both her wicked son and Draco must die. For a scene in which the dragonslayers fire grappling hooks toward the flying dragon, catapults designed to reflect tenth-century engineering were built by the art department. "We shot projectiles from the catapults to represent the grappling hooks," explained Kit West. "Draco catches the grappling hooks and yanks on them; then the catapults are dragged to the castle wall, where they finally go over the sides. We had four big

catapults up on a platform above the castle, with a false wall down one side. We used cranes to drag the catapults across. At the point where the dragon grabs the hooks and drags the catapults, the dragonslayers are squashed against this false wall, the wall collapses and the catapults go over the wall."

Draco is captured only when Einon is struck in the chest with an arrow. Disabled by the sympathetic pain of the hit, Draco falls into the castle courtyard below. "We shot the background for that on location, with David Thewlis in the foreground as we panned up to the castle," Scott Squires noted. "What follows is a shot looking down into the courtyard, where we see Draco being chained up." A computer-generated chain and cleats would augment the real elements shot on location. "There were some cleats in the ground and on the wall, but there weren't enough of them, so we knew we would be adding more in CG." For shots of the chain being wrapped

around Draco's horns, real chain was used in conjunction with the top of the full-size prop head. To suggest the dragon's resistant movement in subsequent shots, a pipe rig was set up to hold a set of chains. Manual movement of the pipe rig would simulate the dragon's struggling, and the resulting rattling chain footage would be married to the CG imagery of Draco.

As Draco is chained in the castle courtyard, Bowen and Einon engage in a long and bitter sword fight that ends in the castle tower. The scene was so boisterous that Dennis Quaid's finger was broken in the course of filming. "On the second take," Quaid recalled, "someone zigged when they should have zagged and I felt cold steel on my finger. I kept going because a

doctor on the set said it wasn't broken—but I knew it wasn't working right. The next morning the bone was sticking up, almost poking out of the skin. So I went to a hospital in Vienna, and it turned out that it was broken in two places. They put a huge cast on it that went clear up to my forearm, but it was dressed and painted black so that you wouldn't see it in the film."

The fight ends with Einon plummeting from a tower window. Bowen then turns his attention to freeing the fallen dragon, mistakenly assuming that Einon is dead. Draco, however, knows that Einon still lives—and will continue to live as long as he himself is alive. Draco implores his friend to kill him, and thus put an end to the evil king. When Bowen refuses and walks away, the dragon shoots flames toward his retreating form in an attempt to make him fight. The fire effects for the shot were achieved practically, and filmed with a long lens to make Quaid appear to be closer to the flames than he actually was. Separate flame elements were also shot and would be composited in later to enhance the scene.

Einon then reappears, intent on murdering Bowen. With an ax raised toward Einon, his former protégé, the knight of the old code suddenly realizes what he must do. He turns quickly and aims the weapon toward Draco's exposed chest. The entire sequence of events was filmed with the camera overcranked to create a slow-motion effect.

"You don't actually see the ax hit the dragon," said John Swallow. "You just see Dennis throw it, and then in the next shot it is there in Draco's chest. Rob didn't want to play it too gruesomely, especially since the dragon was one of the heroes of the movie."

As Draco lies dying, Bowen has his last few moments with the dragon—an emotional scene Quaid played with only a lightstand positioned in the place the CG Draco would eventually be inserted. Their good-byes said, Draco dies, his body gradually disappearing, replaced by a flowing liquid light. To suggest the intensity of the nebulalike apparition—which would be created as a computer-generated element—special computerized lights commonly used at rock-

and-roll concerts were procured by John Swallow and positioned on the set, producing a bright interactive light on the actors' faces. Five of the large lights were mounted together in a kind of star pattern and ramped up as the scene progressed.

A poignant moment added by Cohen on the set was Draco's spirit form reaching out to touch Bowen's cheek. "I felt it was important to have that contact between them at the end," Cohen commented. "Throughout the movie, there has been such disparity between their sizes, Bowen and Draco have not really been able to touch. Draco's hand was so big, they couldn't even shake hands. It is not until Draco is dead and has become this spirit that he can touch his friend. Bowen feels his face being stroked, like the father stroking the son's face before he goes off on his next journey."

With that gesture, the light glow begins to move up over the castle wall and toward the heavens. Kit West's and David Eggby's crews built a three-foot-square light box with translucent material on all sides to hold a number of lighting instruments. That light box, which created a very bright glow, was mounted to a cable strung from one side of the castle courtyard to the other. "They could pull this thing across and up, and you'd see the light moving across the scene and onto the faces of everybody there," Squires said. "It also gave all the actors and extras something to look at and follow with their eyes." In postproduction, the light rig would be replaced with the computer-generated glow of Draco's spirit.

Winter was now upon the country in full force, and with the castle shoot completed, the chilled-to-the-bone actors and crew members eagerly returned to Bratislava, where they would shoot interior scenes on the stages at Koliba Studios for two and a half weeks. The retreat to shel-

ter did not come a moment too soon—a fact that was emphasized when a major snowstorm hit two days after the move.

The company's tenure at the studio included shooting Kara's rape scene in Einon's bed-chamber, her subsequent escape through the cistern and an early scene at the volcanic cave where Draco gives the boy Einon half his dragon's heart. The cave interior was one of the most difficult stage sets to construct, since it had to be rigged to look as if it was simmering with volcanic activity. "We put in all these bubbling vats of lava and steam," noted Kit West. "For the lava we mixed up a formula from a powder commonly used as a thickener for cooking. It is nontoxic, so we didn't have to worry about using it with the actors and crew. We put this mixture in pits on the cave set that we underlit with red-gelled lights. Then we pumped in air to make it bubble, put steam coming up through it and covered it with a kind of black dust to create the lava crust."

For the visual effects crew, the major issue in the cave sequence was the creation of the glowing heartlight that flows from the dragon to the dying boy. Although the flowing light itself would be a computer-generated effect realized in postproduction, the interactive light hitting the faces of the actors had to be achieved on the set. The same computerized lights used in Draco's death scene were employed. "This heartlight was supposed to actually pour into Einon's heart," Squires noted, "effecting a change in Einon as he is healed right before your eyes." The miraculous "healing" was achieved through a CG effect that transitioned from a prosthetic chest wound piece to a prosthetic scar worn by the actor portraying Einon as a boy.

With all of the interiors completed, the film finally wrapped on November 26. For nearly five months, the cast and crew had made the best of what was, in many respects, a taxing experience. Dina Meyer, who at the beginning of the shoot crossed off each long, hard day on a calendar as it passed, had gone on to make several close friends during the production and found herself reluctant to leave Slovakia. Dennis Quaid, who had carried a heavier burden—both literally and figuratively—than any of the other actors, also left with fond memories of the country and his *Dragonheart* colleagues. "Shooting *Dragonheart* was a very monastic experience for me," Quaid commented. "We were in a spot where there was no television, except for CNN. Nobody spoke English. There was only one decent restaurant, so we went to that same place every day for five months. It was not a fun place to make a movie.

"But as difficult as this film was to shoot, and as miserable as the conditions were, Rob always had incredible passion for it—and that fired us up and got us through it. I think I would

have shot myself if it hadn't been for that. We really bonded over there. All of us were buoyed by the belief that this film was very special—and that feeling is still with me. *Dragonheart* will always hold a special place in my heart, no matter what it does at the box office."

The production phase of making the movie, while challenging, had gone off without a hitch—and had even come in ahead of schedule and under budget. Eastern Europe had provided Cohen and de Laurentiis with the means to shoot their long-nurtured project as economically as possible; and yet, no compromises had been required. "We had a fabulous experience working in Slovakia," de Laurentiis enthused. "They had good technicians, they had horses and castles and swords—everything we needed. I've been producing movies for seventeen years, and most of them have been made in foreign locations. I've worked in Mexico, in mainland China, all over Europe—but I've never had as good an experience as I did in Eastern Europe."

Cohen and de Laurentiis returned to Los Angeles with what was, in many respects, a completed movie. "What I was most proud of after we had finished shooting the live-action," said Cohen, "was that the story was enjoyable and touching as it was—even though Dennis, at that point, was only acting against tennis balls. I knew we had something really wonderful in the live-action, and my main thought as we entered postproduction was, 'Now, if we can just not screw up this last leg . . .' In order to make *Dragonheart* a reality, we had to be able to come up with a Draco that was real and emotive and spectacular."

Five hundred miles north of Los Angeles, in San Rafael, California, Scott Squires, Judith Weaver and a team of visual effects artisans were gearing up to do just that.

POSTPRODUCTION

"It was an entire movie with the main character talking to air—
but it was still so beautiful and wonderful, I teared up at the end."
— Raffaella de Laurentiis

It had been an uncommonly long and arduous shoot, and when Raffaella de Laurentiis, Rob Cohen and their crew returned to the United States at the end of November, they gratefully gave themselves up to the recuperation of the Christmas break. They were home, and they had in their possession reels of footage on which had been captured boisterous battle scenes, breathtakingly beautiful vistas, spirited, poignant and humorous scenes

between the principal actors, spectacular explosions and an entire world that seemed to have sprung from the Dark Ages, complete with authentic architecture and an array of convincing tenth-century trappings. Most significantly, they had on celluloid, through Dennis Quaid's performance, half of the central relationship around which the entire movie revolved.

What they did *not* have was Draco. The decision to achieve all of the Draco CG shots in a yearlong postproduction had been an unusual one. Typically, big effects movies are structured to enable the effects team to work more or less concurrently with the production unit, with effects shots delivered three to six months after principal photography has wrapped. While the advantage of this standard sequence of events is that even a complex effects film can be completed in approximately one year, the common drawback is that costly effects shots are realized, only to be excised from the film in its final edited form.

Wisely, de Laurentiis and Cohen had suggested a different structure. "Originally, the studio wanted the film for summer 1995," de Laurentiis explained. "That would have meant that we shot through the summer and fall of 1994, delivering scenes as they were shot to ILM. ILM would complete the CG shots accordingly, working on them as production continued. But because we had such an enormous number of CG shots, I didn't think there was any way they could get them done that quickly. It would have been a struggle even to get the movie done for a Christmas 1995 release. So at a big meeting with the studio I suggested that we aim for a summer 1996 release; that we shoot the movie in its entirety, without giving ILM anything. After the movie was shot, Rob could cut it and edit all the plates in, just as if the dragon was there. In essence, he would have the final cut of the movie. Then, once the picture was locked, we would give it to ILM and they would still have a full year in which to complete their shots."

After some initial hesitation, the studio eventually conceded that the plan was a good one. "We literally saved millions of dollars by doing it this way," de Laurentiis asserted. "When ILM started their work, we had a picture that was completely edited and finished. It was an hour and fifty-eight minutes long, and it was the movie that would be going out to theaters. So we knew at that point exactly what dragon shots had to be done, and the margin of error was greatly reduced. If we had done it the other way, ILM would have created shots—at the cost of hundreds of thousands of dollars—for scenes that didn't wind up in the movie anyway."

Although the actual generation of visual effects shots would not commence until the film had been edited, Judith Weaver and CG supervisors Alex Seiden and Evan MacDonald had been working full-time on *Dragonheart* throughout production, looking over plates as they were completed and readying their team for the large-scale CG effort. "We were getting plates from Slovakia throughout the shoot," Seiden recalled. "Judith and I would take a look at them as they came in to make sure that everything was going smoothly and that the data we were getting was usable. We would also talk to Scott Squires via E-mail or the occasional tortured transatlantic call to keep up on what was happening over there."

As production segued into postproduction, the CG team began to address the specifics of how Draco would be created. While the preceding decade had seen a tremendous advance in the sophistication of digital technology, the basic techniques for realizing CG characters had remained essentially unchanged since ILM had first computer-generated a stained-glass knight leaping from a church window for 1985's *Young Sherlock Holmes*.

The process begins with the "building" of a wire-frame computer model, either from scratch or through the scanning-in of a three-dimensional sculpture. Typically, the wire-frame model is built in separate body sections, then joined together through specific software programs. Animation is achieved by the movement of the points, or control vertices, which make up the model. When the animation is completed, the wire-frame is finally rendered as a fully colored and textured form. Lighting effects such as highlights and shadows are also rendered to complete the CG character and make it blend convincingly with the live-action background.

While research and development for the *Dragonheart* project was ongoing at ILM, none of these steps in achieving the computer-generated dragon could be implemented until the final cut of the film had been delivered. The job of shaping Cohen's reels of footage into a polished, finalized film fell to editor Peter Amundsen. Cohen had collaborated with the editor several times during his years as a producer, and it was Amundsen who had edited *Dragon: The Bruce Lee Story*. "The great thing about Peter," Cohen stated, "is that he is so honest with you. He is extremely articulate in explaining his decisions and suggestions. He is also very structurally oriented, yet one of the most inventive editors I've ever known."

Amundsen's work on the film had actually begun long before the crew's return to the

United States. Throughout the shoot in Slovakia, the editor had labored at the editing suites on the Universal lot, assembling shots as they were completed and shipped and making his suggestions through phone or fax.

While it is common for an editor to work side by side with a film's director throughout principal photography, Cohen had preferred to keep the editing process separate from the daily grind of filming. "I didn't want Peter to be with us on location," Cohen explained, "because I didn't want him to know how hard things were. I felt it would only compromise his decision-making capabilities. If you see a bunch of people suffering to make a particular scene, you are going to be reluctant to go to the director and say, 'It isn't working.' On location, we suffered. There was terrible heat and terrible cold; Dennis broke his finger; the horse threw him a million times—the horrors went on and on and on. But why should the editor see all of that? Why should he watch a bunch of exhausted, sunburned, windburned, dehydrated people trudging into dailies each night? It would only hurt his objectivity. What I needed from Peter was his ability to look at a scene and decide if it was good or not good, engaging or boring, without any thought as to how difficult it had been for us to film it."

Cohen's other reason for keeping Amundsen in Los Angeles through the production schedule was that the director did not want to see how the rough cut was coming together until *after* filming had wrapped. "I don't like to go into the editing room during production," Cohen said. "I look at dailies, of course, but I don't like to see any kind of rough cut while I am filming. During filming, I am still living with the *dream* of what the movie is; I don't want to know yet what the reality is. To go out there every day on the shoot, you have to believe that your dream is coming true. I told Peter that if the shots he was getting were off-base in some way, he should let me know; but other than that, I just wanted him to edit the movie as he saw fit."

On January 9, 1995, Amundsen gave Cohen a two-hour-and-eighteen-minute first cut. "Peter's first cut of *Dragonheart* was very good and completely coherent," Cohen said. "It may not have been exactly what I would have done, but fifty percent of it was *better* than what I would have done. I never tell an editor how to cut that first one—that one is his. I want to know how *he* thinks the material should go together. I can always change things if I want to afterward."

At this point, with a first cut in hand, Cohen and Amundsen sat down together and began going through the film reel by reel. "I looked at what Peter had done in his cut and made suggestions," Cohen recalled. "We worked our way through each reel that way, tightening things up as we went along. By the time we had worked through all the reels, we were down to about two hours and seven minutes."

One of the scenes cut from the film was Bowen's and Kara's declarations of love for each other. As scripted, the scene had come as Bowen's makeshift troops prepare to storm Einon's castle. "A movie tells you what it wants and what it doesn't want," Cohen observed, "and this movie didn't want that love scene. I had shot it, and it was cut into the movie, but when I saw it, it seemed all wrong. The love story didn't suit Kara's character at all. In the scene, Kara refers to the fact that she has been raped by Einon and that, as a result, she doesn't have anything to give Bowen. As I watched it, I thought, 'This isn't Kara! Kara wants to use a Viking ax and chop off some heads and get her people free, or die trying! This isn't a girl who is going to stand around giving this kind of sappy speech.'"

In addition to the cutting of superfluous scenes and shots, another task that was executed during this phase of the editing was the scene-by-scene replacement of Rob Cohen's voice as Draco—as recorded on the set—with Sean Connery's original recorded performance. "It was a great relief to me and everyone else when we started putting Sean's voice back into the film," Cohen laughed. "After we had the film edited, we showed it to Sean, and then did a second recording in Rome. But approximately sixty-five percent of the final voice performance was from the first session, because Sean had done a great job to begin with. There were little technical things that had to be changed due to slight revisions in the script or changes that had been made in scenes on location. For instance, the old scarred dragon had originally been a male, and now was a female, so we had to change the 'he's' to 'she's.'" A third recording session was done to tune up the lip-syncing of specific lines of dialogue once all of the CG Draco shots had been inserted.

After Cohen and Amundsen had refined the scenes reel by reel, it was time for the director to look at the film as a whole for the first time. This viewing would reveal what subtle refinements still needed to be made. "I was looking for continuity problems, such as too many shots in a row where people were panting, or too little visual variety from shot to shot. I was also concerned with issues of rhythm, how loosely or tightly things were cut. To determine all those things, I had to look at the movie as a whole, rather than separate scenes. From that screening I was able to see if this string of beads was making a necklace."

Up to this point in the editing process, producer Raffaella de Laurentiis had not yet viewed the film. "Raffaella's objectivity was the most valuable thing I had going for me," Cohen explained, "so I didn't want to squander it too early. I knew that when I had worked on the movie until I was blind and couldn't see one more thing to do, she would see tons of stuff to do. So I worked and worked with Peter until we had it to a good length, about two hours, and I couldn't see one more thing to change or cut." Only when the film was edited to his satisfaction was Cohen finally ready to screen it for de Laurentiis, the woman who had nurtured the project from its infancy. "It was a very nervous screening for me," Cohen admitted, "because Raffaella's opinion was the one I cared the most about. She is not only my producer and my partner, she is like my sister—we are family. Not only that, this was *her* baby. I was just the midwife. I couldn't have borne it to look in her eyes and see disappointment."

He need not have feared. Armed with a pad for the taking of notes, de Laurentiis sat down in a small theater on the Universal lot to see *Dragonheart* for the first time. The producer was nothing less than ecstatic over what she saw projected on the big screen. "Of course, I was terrified to see this first cut," she recalled. "But I was so moved by it! It was an entire movie with the main character talking to air—but it was still so beautiful and wonderful, I teared up at the end."

> *"We went in, and we sat there watching the test—and nobody said anything for the first couple of minutes. It was terrible. Scott and I were thinking, 'Oh, my God, don't they like it?'"*
> —Judith Weaver

By the middle of March 1995, Cohen and Amundsen had finessed the rough footage into a polished film. With the editing task completed, the time had finally come to turn *Dragonheart* over to Industrial Light & Magic, where 182 CG shots—making up twenty-five minutes of film time—would be realized. Rather than directing actors on a set or guiding the production design and cinematography, Cohen's responsibilities now centered on steering a team of twenty animators through the process of executing a credible dragon performance. "This was a very complex thing we were trying to pull off," Cohen observed. "We were attempting to create a CG character that could perform and make the audience feel an emotional response. To do that, we all had to be thinking along the same lines. It wasn't like directing actors, where I could do as many takes as I needed to get the performance I wanted. These CG shots were expensive and time-consuming, so they had to be right the first time."

Communication between the ILM team and Cohen—separated by nearly five hundred miles—was facilitated through a fiber-optic hookup that enabled the CG team to feed images directly to a monitor in Cohen's Universal Studios office. "The fiber optic link allowed me to see shots progress every day," Cohen said. "It kept me in touch with ILM in a way I couldn't have been through phone conversations or faxed messages alone." Cohen also made several trips to the San Rafael facility to meet with Scott Squires and the entire crew. Many such sessions were videotaped so that Cohen's directions could be referred to long after the director had returned to Los Angeles. "The animating and technical directing staff at ILM was going to be growing as postproduction moved along," Cohen explained. "These videotapes were a way for all the new people to get up to speed quickly. I didn't want to keep going back to the beginning, explaining over and over again what every scene meant or what I wanted for specific shots."

Another tool Cohen conceived of to aid ILM in the creation of Draco's performance was a huge reference library of footage from Sean Connery's previous film work. Culling through Connery's extensive filmography, Cohen edited key performance moments, assembling hundreds of images that the animators could use as a guide in devising the dragon's various expressions and moods. "Sean has an incredible body of work," Cohen observed, "and I was able to pull from all of those films, from the beginning of his career to his most recent performances. I categorized every possible emotion, and we ended up with shots of Connery sardonic, amused, skeptical, critical, charming, seductive, intellectual, introspective, melancholy. We broke down his emotional life and studied how he uses his eyes and posture and body. We analyzed his performances very carefully and tried to translate them to Draco. It was extremely helpful, because it gave the animators something to look at when they were trying to make Draco look angry, for example. I could tell them, 'Go to the anger bin and you will see something Sean does in *Russia House*—that's what I want for Draco in this moment.' Instead of just saying, 'I want Draco to be angry,' I had something to give them so that they would know exactly what I wanted."

With reference footage and the completed film in their hands, the members of ILM's digital department set out to meet the incredible challenge of creating *Dragonheart's* main character entirely within the virtual realm. "There were many, many difficulties in creating this character that none of us had ever faced before," Squires said. "For one thing, most of the shots were very long, and most of them had dialogue. They weren't short little clips of a creature running through darkness, which is the kind of cheat you typically see in a creature movie.

"Another problem was that we were constantly going back and forth between Draco and the other characters in the film, *or* we were seeing them together in the same scene. So there was always a direct comparison: Here is reality; here is nonreality. We had to make a dragon that could hold up to that comparison. You would think there would be more freedom in doing a dragon, because it is a mythical creature and nobody knows what it looks like anyway; but the fact that it was a fantasy creature actually made our job harder. We were given this fantastic design, this creature that was obviously fantasy-based, but we had to make it look as if it was reality-based. At least with an animal you have that animal as reference; for Draco, we had nothing to rely on but Phil Tippett's design instincts and our own instincts."

The CG team began the process of generating its dragon character with the building of the computer model. The five-foot-long dragon maquette—supplied by the Tippett Studio—had been cut up into sections that were individually scanned into the computer to provide the CG team with a rough version of the final model. "The scan gave us a starting point," noted Judith Weaver, "but there was still a lot of work to do before we had a workable model. This dragon was by far the most complicated and elaborate computer model we had ever built. The

T-rex in *Jurassic Park* had about seven or eight thousand control vertices; Draco had four times that many, about thirty thousand. Phil Tippett really threw down the gauntlet with this design: 'You think you're so tough? Here, build this!'"

Because the CG team had to build the model as quickly as possible to meet its schedule, four different modelers were each given a separate part of the body to construct. "We hoped that the parts would all come together and meet in the middle," said Weaver. "And with some tweaking and refining, they did."

Once the complex model was finalized, Squires and animation supervisor James Straus addressed some of the inherent animation problems. "We were very well aware of the fact that we had to get the audience to a point where they didn't think about Draco as an effect," Squires said. "That meant that we had to push even harder, technologically and creatively. We were trying to sell Draco as a character—a real, emotive character that people would believe in. What made that so difficult was that this wasn't just a dragon, it was a *talking* dragon! He was also a passionate, feeling dragon, a funny, happy, sad dragon. And as if that wasn't hard enough, he also had to be this magical character who was made of starlight and could fly upside down. The laws of physics—which we rely on in producing animation that looks believable—were just thrown out the window with this character."

Specific animation problems included the complex folding and unfolding of the wings, as well as the movement of the armorlike scales against each other as the dragon moved. Another major issue for the animators was the amount of dialogue the character would be required to speak. Whereas the dinosaurs in *Jurassic Park* had been required only to snarl or roar, Draco would have to move his mouth in a convincing fashion to match Sean Connery's recorded dialogue. A related problem was the execution of extremely subtle facial animation. "This was a main character that had to act," noted Seiden, "so we jumped into working out our approach for the lip-sync and facial animation. It was a big challenge to make a creature talk and not have him look like Mr. Ed. We had about a dozen people get together to brainstorm, and we came out of that with a set of techniques and tools to use."

Among those tools was a program—dubbed "Caricature"—written by software programmer Cary Phillips. "On previous projects," said Weaver, "we had animated lip-sync by moving one point of the model at a time. But that would have been terribly labor-intensive for this project. There was just too much dialogue in this movie to try to do it that way. We had a similar problem in the facial expression, since Draco had to show such a wide range of emotion. So we decided we had to come up with a new way of doing things. We sat down with James Straus and asked him what would be his ideal method of animating, if he could do it any way he wanted. His response was that he would want to animate with *shapes* rather than points—but we didn't have a real facile program for doing that. So Cary wrote the Caricature program, which we used with Softimage—our standard animation program—to animate all the lip-sync and facial animation. This program simulated musculature, in a way, because it created shapes inside the face that could be animated. Another advantage to it was that the animators could use it in real time, so they could see right away what they were getting."

Throughout the animation process, the dragon was either in wire-frame or shaded form. It was not until the rendering phase that the model was endowed with the spiked, scaled texture and wild color palette Tippett's team had devised in their maquettes. Digital artist Carolyn Rendu

was responsible for replicating the look in a series of computer-painted texture maps that were essentially wrapped onto the wire-frame image. "Phil's color scheme made the dragon look very magical and wonderful," Weaver noted, "but it posed another challenge in making Draco appear to be a real creature because it was so fantastic. Carolyn did a great job of duplicating the original design." Painting files—done in Viewpaint, ILM's paint program—were combined with animation files by the technical directors (TDs), whose job it was to render the final character. "Once they had everything rendered, the TDs began to determine how the character needed to be lit from shot to shot."

Lighting a CG character is done by setting up virtual lights within the computer to simulate on-set lighting conditions. To simplify the task, Squires had filmed lighting reference on location, photographing a white card held up where Draco would be in the shot to see how the lights fell on it, as well as their color and intensity. Both the reference footage and meticulous records regarding all aspects of the lighting were sent back to ILM and referred to frequently by the technical directors.

Equipped with reference from the shoot, the Caricature program and, most significantly, years of visual and digital effects experience, Squires and his team first committed themselves to producing a test shot for Cohen's and de Laurentiis's approval. For their test, Squires and Weaver decided to realize a shot of Draco at the waterfall with Kara. The shot encompassed nearly all of the inherent difficulties of creating the computer-generated character. "We felt the

waterfall scene with Kara was a good starting place," Squires said, "because it covered a number of key issues without getting into the heavier technical problems. It was a relatively short scene, but it entailed dialogue and expression changes. Because it was a daylight shot, it also required that we work out the lighting problems we would be facing. Most CG packages don't do outdoor lighting correctly, so we had to be creative in how we lit the shot."

The scene also presented the problem of creating the interaction of water hitting against Draco's legs as he stood at the base of the waterfall. "We had used full-size black legs on the set to get some interaction, but that technique didn't work very well. For our test, we removed those black legs from the plate, took a little bit of the ripple wave action from a rock that was there and used that for the interaction on Draco's legs. We also shot some additional water elements for a shot of Draco moving his arm across the water. There was a lot to do on this scene."

Near the end of April 1995, Cohen and de Laurentiis flew to San Rafael to see ILM's completed test. Both had all the confidence in the world in the company, and yet, both felt a palpable anxiety as they made their way north. This was, in many respects, the moment of truth for *Dragonheart*. Despite all their efforts, the filmmakers knew, if Draco was not real, if he did not come off with all the charm and depth and feeling of the scripted character, if he did not appear to be, as Cohen had put it, "mythic and glorious," then all was lost.

Upon their arrival, pleasantries were quickly exchanged, then de Laurentiis urged that they go immediately to ILM's state-of-the-art screening theater to see the test. "I had worked on this project for seven years," de Laurentiis said, "so I had a lot of anxiety about seeing this first test shot. All I could think was, 'What if this doesn't work?'"

"Raffaella was very nervous when she came in," Judith Weaver confirmed. "She didn't want to chat at all; she just wanted to go in and see the test immediately. We went in, and we sat there watching the test—and nobody said anything for the first couple of minutes. It was terrible. Scott and I were thinking, 'Oh, my God, don't they like it?' Finally, Raffaella said, 'I can't believe this. I think I'm going to cry.' Rob was also very pleased. He noticed all the nuances we'd put in, such as the tongue rolling with Sean Connery's Scottish burr. Their reaction was very gratifying to us."

"I was so amazed when they ran the shot, I couldn't even speak," de Laurentiis said. "I just flipped. There was Draco, in broad daylight—which everyone had told me couldn't be done—and he was fabulous. It was very exciting."

While the test was a resounding success, ILM still had months of work ahead of it, and many Draco riddles to decipher. Flying shots, which Squires had determined would be among the most difficult to execute, were left to the end of the CG schedule. "I thought it was best to save the harder stuff for the end," Squires explained, "after we'd had some time to get up and running and to become familiar with the difficulties in doing this character."

Among the shots tackled at the beginning of the schedule was one in which Draco offers his heart to Einon. Set in the volcanic cave, the scene is played almost entirely from Draco's point of view, and the dragon is not revealed until the end. Even then, his image is brief and dimly lit. In addition to rendering a Draco silhouette, the ILM team had to create the glow of the heartlight—which Cohen had described as "liquid light"—and composite flame elements that had been shot separately.

As the effort progressed—and the team's confidence and proficiency in realizing the character grew—some of the more demanding shots, including those in the aerial sequences, were approached. "The key issue with the flying shots was that Draco had these articulated wings," Squires explained. "They had to look just right as they moved, as if the air was catching them from underneath. The other problem was figuring out how the wings would fold up and unfold, which was a very complicated set of moves. We wound up doing a lot of testing and research and development to get the wings and flying to look right."

The first shot of Draco in flight follows his confrontation with Bowen at the waterfall. Bursting out from behind the water, Draco becomes airborne as Bowen fires a bolo into the air and catches the fly-

ing dragon by the foot. Not only did ILM have to create the shots of the flying dragon, the bolo was also computer generated. "We have a down-shot of the bolo approaching," said Squires, "then we cut to profile shots of Draco flying as the bolo grabs his foot. Aerial plates for that sequence had been shot from the microlight, so we had a lot of footage from Draco's POV that we were able to utilize."

Draco then swoops down to pick Bowen up in his mouth. "For that shot we replaced Dennis Quaid with a little CG man," said Squires. "Then, once Bowen was in the mouth, we cut to the mechanical jaw and tongue we had used on location." Markers—actually Ping-Pong balls cut in half—had been placed on the side of the full-scale jaw to guide the digital artists when it came time to marry the CG imagery of the head to the animatronic device. "We had to plot all of that action so that the CG head would appear to be part of the practical rig," Squires explained. "We took detailed measurements on location, and carefully recorded the placement of the practical head, so that we would know from a CG standpoint what the action was and what the camera was doing throughout the scene. Because we had cheated the scale of the rig a bit in order to get Dennis Quaid to fit inside the jaw comfortably, we had to scale the CG head up accordingly. Once it was finalized, we tracked the CG head to the live-action jaw frame by frame."

One of the last shots to be attempted by ILM was Draco's aerial approach of Avalon. In the story, the dragon has rescued Kara, Bowen and Gilbert from the angry mob of swamp villagers, picking them up—horse and all—and flying off to the tor haven. "In the approach shot," noted Squires, "you see Draco flying with the three of them on this little horse. All the characters in that shot were computer-generated. We were able to get away with that because it was a distant shot and the camera didn't linger on it for too long."

Another sequence that was realized as ILM's deadline drew near was Draco's death scene at the end of the film. The scene was complicated somewhat by the close proximity of Bowen and Draco—a live character and a CG character—as they exchange lines of dialogue. Throughout most of the film, Cohen had deliberately kept the physical interaction between Draco and the human characters to a minimum. Not only did the limited contact simplify the CG process, it also pointed out, with some poignancy, the physical disparity between Draco and Bowen and the consequently awkward nature of their relationship. It was not until the end of the film, when Draco is captured and chained in the castle courtyard, that Bowen and his giant friend would have much in the way of physical contact. "Throughout that scene," said Squires, "Bowen and Draco speak to each other in close-up. Because Draco is chained down, Bowen is able to get right in front of his face to talk to him. So we had to cast a shadow from Bowen onto Draco, and from Draco onto Bowen. There is also a point in the scene where Draco is trying to make Bowen fight, so he reaches out to smack him. Working out the timing of that interaction was very tricky."

A CG effect for the end sequence that had not been originally scheduled or budgeted was the re-creation of the vaporous breath that could be seen emanating from all of the live-action characters. "It was so cold at the castle when we shot the live-action there, you could see everyone's breath as they spoke," Squires said. "So, naturally, we had to do the same for Draco. We created a CG vapor to come out of his mouth every time he spoke. It was an added problem we hadn't counted on, and it made these final scenes much more difficult."

The film's ending also required a computer-generated Draco constellation and a glorious stellar ballet for shots of the dragon ascending to the heavens after his death. The sequence begins with a shot of Draco's glowing spirit form moving toward the stars. In the following series of shots, the light becomes a star shape and meets up with other stars in the constellation. "Those stars gather around Draco's spirit, as if they are greeting him," Squires

explained. "Then there is a kind of explosion, a fireworks display, and we cut back to a close-up of Bowen. It is an extreme close-up on his eyes; and there in his eyes we see the reflection of this starburst.

"After the starburst we see a shimmering vision of Draco's head in the display, then the stardust coalesces into stars which move back into their constellation form. At that point, Draco's head is one of the stars, which is just a little bit different in color. The star seems to blink, as if Draco is winking to Bowen and signifying that this is where he wants to be. That entire sequence was created digitally." A simplified foreshadowing of Draco's spectacular ascent to the stars is seen in his campfire scene with Bowen earlier in the film. The Draco constellation was computer-generated for the scene, as was an outline of the dragon's form in blue stardust.

Less magical—but in some instances, just as difficult—were those mundane objects which, due to their direct interaction with Draco, also had to be computer-generated. Arrows shot from Bowen's whacker and caught in the pit of Draco's wing, for example, were all rendered digitally. Likewise, a number of props used in the film's finale had to be replicated in the computer. Shots of Draco being captured by the team of dragonslayers as the peasants battle Einon's men featured CG grappling hooks and rope. "We see Draco flying over the heads of the dragonslayers," Squires explained, "just as they are shooting these grappling hooks. We shot all those sky plates on location, then composited in computer-animated hooks. The production sent us the actual props they had used on location so we could copy them exactly in the CG models. The scene continues with Draco yanking on the rope attached to the hooks; so we had to animate the rope flying in the air and make it look real. That kind of CG effect seems so insignificant against something like Draco—but those kinds of things are really very difficult to do. Everyone knows exactly what rope looks like, so we couldn't get away with anything that wasn't completely realistic."

In addition to producing all of the CG elements, ILM was also charged with a number of related visual effects shots. On its slate was the shooting and tracking of fire elements that

would visually connect Draco's fire-breathing nostrils to the practical fire effects and explosions on the ground. Additional water elements also had to be shot and tracked to appear as if they were interacting with the CG dragon, who spent a great deal of screen time swimming, splashing, standing or running in a variety of ponds, lakes and rivers. Other shots, such as those of Bowen's flight through the forest, required the digital removal of wire rigs and harnesses.

All of ILM's CG and visual effects chores for *Dragonheart* were completed by the time the March 1996 deadline rolled around. As the venerated company had done many times before, ILM had pushed the envelope of digital applications by creating one of the most complex and magical creatures ever to grace a movie screen. In a sense, the project had required a return to the classroom, not only for Rob Cohen, but also for the knowledgeable and experienced effects veterans. "There was a huge learning curve on this project that we all experienced," said Weaver. "But no one had to learn more, and learn it more quickly, than Rob. Fortunately, he was a very quick study. He was open to learning about this technology, and he instinctively grasped what it was he needed to know in order to keep things moving forward. From our perspective, that made him a dream director."

With the compositing of all the Draco shots, *Dragonheart* was, at last, nearly whole. In fact, the only postproduction tasks remaining were the scoring of the film and the creation of a final sound mix, which would include a variety of special sound effects. To Cohen, both the music and the sound were critical to the film's ultimate success. "Music and sound are the two elements that you can bring to your picture at the end that will either lift it or defeat it," Cohen observed. "They are essential. Sound gives you the immediate, vivid context for the story; music gives you the emotional resonance. It is trite to say it, but music is the international language. Schopenhauer said that music is the highest form of art, because it completely bypasses the intellect and goes directly to the soul. I think that is true. A movie, by its nature, has a lot of intellectual elements—it is a story, and you have to use your mind to follow that story—but it is a movie's music that works on your emotional level."

Composer Randy Edelman, who had composed the beautiful, haunting scores for *Dragon* and *The Last of the Mohicans,* was engaged to provide that crucial musical backdrop for *Dragonheart.* "In Randy, I met the guy who speaks the musical language I love," Cohen said. "He finds melody important—he doesn't just come up with a bunch of overorchestrated sounds. He knows how to reinforce a story theme. He is also as comfortable in the electronic world as he is in the symphonic world. That was important to me, because there were some elements of the film that needed a unique sound that you couldn't get through normal classical instruments; but there were other places where we needed the sweep and scale of a symphony orchestra."

Edelman began composing his *Dragonheart* score in late-fall 1995, and by the beginning of the new year the score had been completed and inserted into the film's final sound track. With the addition of the score, the movie had finally found its own, distinctive voice. "Before we had the musical score," Cohen noted, "we had been screening the movie with temporary sound tracks. We had John Williams' music from *Jurassic Park,* James Horner's score from *Far and Away*—there was all this different music that had been thrown together, so the movie didn't have a personal signature. But with Randy's score, the movie finally had music that was specifically tailored to it. It was the difference between an off-the-rack suit and a custom-made suit from Savile Row. Randy is definitely a Savile Row guy—you get that suit, and it is great material and it fits perfectly."

Intertwined with the score in the final mix were sound effects, which are traditionally the responsibility of a sound designer. Much of the sound designer's assignment involved the creation of sounds that would aurally support the tenth-century environment the art department had endeavored to create visually. The distinctive pounding of horses and the sharp clanging of swords and armor in battle were key to the story—yet little of that appropriate din had been captured on location. The kinds of highly directional microphones typically used during filming are great for recording actors' voices, but exclude nearly everything else. "Those microphones are designed to pick up the voices while eliminating extraneous noise," Cohen explained. "The result is that the entire world of sound, other than voices, is lost in your production track and you have to re-create it. It is especially tricky now, because today's audiences have become very sound-savvy. They are accustomed to listening to high-quality stereo in their music, CDs and television, and they expect nothing less in their movie theaters."

In addition to re-creating all of the standard sounds not present in the production sound track, the sound designer had to invent a variety of unusual sound effects specifically for the character of Draco. "We had to figure out how a dragon's body would sound when it moved," Cohen said. "What would all those scales moving against each other sound like? What would his heavy breathing sound like? Draco sings in a scene with Kara, so we also had to conceive of a sound for a dragon's song. It could be like the song of a humpback whale, for example, or something entirely different." Inspiration for the dragon's song hit one day as Cohen watched his young son and his friends as they swam and played on water slides. "There was all this children's laughter, and I thought, 'What if we sampled children's laughter and slowed it down and made that the basis of the dragon's song?' It would be a human sound, but also otherworldly and joyful."

Another unusual and challenging aspect of the sound effects assignment was the prayers of the knights which haunt Bowen at Avalon. "That was a very specialized sound that wasn't able to be pulled from a sound effects library," Cohen noted. "First we had to decide what all of these prayers for courage beaming into Avalon would sound like. Once we had an idea, we recorded fifty or so people speaking in Latin and other languages, and put those all together in an interesting way."

> *"We had to figure out how a dragon's body would sound when it moved. What would all those scales moving against each other sound like?"*
> —Rob Cohen

When both the music and the sound effects had been added to the sound mix, the film was ready for looping—the rerecording of specific lines of dialogue. While nearly every film requires some looping to create a clean sound track, it is particularly useful in effects films that employ noisy Vistavision cameras. The distracting hum of the cameras could be heard in many of *Dragonheart*'s scenes, and as a result, virtually all the principal actors were scheduled for looping sessions at the end of March. "The scene inside the volcanic cave was also a problem, because there was the sound of steam jets and other practical effects that ruined the sound track," said Cohen. "Sound technicians were able to filter out a lot of that extraneous noise with various electronic tricks, but in some cases we had to resort to looping. I didn't really mind, because it gave me a chance to see all of those wonderful actors again. It also gave us a chance to tune up some of the performances a little bit."

Spring 1996 marked both a beginning and an ending for *Dragonheart*. For those involved in the publicity machinery at Universal Pictures, it was the beginning of a weeks-long flurry of trailers, press releases and television and billboard advertising, all intended to inform summer movie audiences that a new film "created by the visual effects wizards who brought you *Jurassic Park*" was about to be released.

For Rob Cohen and Raffaella de Laurentiis, however, *Dragonheart* had come to an end.

The filmmakers had admirably fulfilled all of their obligations to the film; and as thousands of prints were being made, there was nothing left to do but wait and see if the story that had captured their imaginations so long ago would have a similar impact on the moviegoing public.

Although both the director and the producer had high hopes for the film's performance at the box office, their deepest personal rewards had been reaped the moment the completed film had first threaded its way through a movie projector. "I don't think I will ever do anything again that I will love as much as *Dragonheart*," de Laurentiis reflected. "In some ways, that is a difficult thing to realize. I invested eight years of my life in this movie, and I never once lost my enthusiasm and love for it. I knew I would eventually get this movie made. The great thing was that I got it made my way, with people I love."

Rob Cohen had not carried the project in his heart for as long as de Laurentiis, but the experience of making the film was no less meaningful to him. "As a director, this project stretched my imagination tremendously. I had always done reality-based action films, and in those kinds of films, you have only your own experience to draw upon. Doing a film that takes place in the tenth century, in the world of dragons and knights, pulled me out of reality and into the realm of fantasy. It was a real growth experience for me professionally.

"But it also was a growing experience personally. The most important elements of this story, to me, were the spiritual aspects of it. To prepare for this movie, I did a lot of reading and contemplating, and I got in touch with spiritual aspects of myself that I didn't know I had. Years ago, when I first read this script, I saw it as a wonderful adventure story; but then my own life experience opened my eyes to its deeper possibilities. If you are lucky, you get to a place in your career where technical dexterity meets a full heart. With *Dragonheart*, I think I got to that place."

> *"If you are lucky, you get to a place in your career where technical dexterity meets a full heart."*
> —Rob Cohen

JODY DUNCAN is the editor of *Cinefex* magazine, a journal covering special and visual effects. She is the author of a book on the making of *The Flintstones*, and with Don Shay wrote the best-selling *The Making of Jurassic Park* and *The Making of Terminator 2: Judgment Day*. With Janine Pourroy, she also wrote *The Making of Congo*. In addition to her film-related work, Ms. Duncan authored *A Warring Absence*, a national award–winning play.

DRAGONHEART

UNIVERSAL PICTURES PRESENTS A RAFFAELLA DE LAURENTIIS PRODUCTION A ROB COHEN FILM

DENNIS QUAID

"DRAGONHEART" DAVID THEWLIS PETE POSTLETHWAITE DINA MEYER WITH JULIE CHRISTIE

AND SEAN CONNERY AS DRACO

MUSIC BY RANDY EDELMAN   SPECIAL VISUAL EFFECTS AND ANIMATION BY INDUSTRIAL LIGHT & MAGIC   VISUAL EFFECTS SUPERVISOR SCOTT SQUIRES

DRAGON DESIGNS BY PHIL TIPPETT   CO-PRODUCER HESTER HARGETT   EFFECTS PRODUCER JOHN SWALLOW   EDITOR PETER AMUNDSON

PRODUCTION DESIGNER BENJAMIN FERNANDEZ   DIRECTOR OF PHOTOGRAPHY DAVID EGGBY A.C.S.

EXECUTIVE PRODUCERS DAVID ROTMAN PATRICK READ JOHNSON

STORY BY PATRICK READ JOHNSON & CHARLES EDWARD POGUE   SCREENPLAY BY CHARLES EDWARD POGUE

PRODUCED BY RAFFAELLA DE LAURENTIIS

DIRECTED BY ROB COHEN

YOU WILL BELIEVE.